Python Programming

Complete Crash Course For Becoming an Expert at Python

Nick Goddard

Legal & Disclaimer

Legal & Disclaimer

This document is geared towards providing exact and reliable information in
regards to the topic and issue covered. The publication is sold with the idea
that the publisher is not required to render accounting, officially permitted, or
otherwise, qualified services. If advice is necessary, legal or professional, a
practiced individual in the profession should be ordered.

- From a Declaration of Principles which was accepted and approved equally
by a Committee of the American Bar Association and a Committee of
Publishers and Associations.

In no way is it legal to reproduce, duplicate, or transmit any part of this
document in either electronic means or in printed format. Recording of this
publication is strictly prohibited and any storage of this document is not
allowed unless with written permission from the publisher. All rights
reserved.

The information provided herein is stated to be truthful and consistent, in that
any liability, in terms of inattention or otherwise, by any usage or abuse of
any policies, processes, or directions contained within is the solitary and utter
responsibility of the recipient reader. Under no circumstances will any legal
responsibility or blame be held against the publisher for any reparation,

Table of Contents

Introduction

Chapter 1 : Introduction to Python Programming Language

Chapter 2: Installation and Environment Setup.

Chapter 3: Syntax used in Python.

Chapter 4: Variable Types

Chapter 5: Operators

Chapter 6: Loops

Chapter 7: Decision Making

Chapter 8: Python in-Built Strings and Numbers Functions.

Chapter 9: Use of Lists

Chapter 10: Use of Tuples

Chapter 11: Use of Dictionary

Chapter 12: Date and Time Function

Chapter 13: Use of Functions

Chapter 14: Use of Modules

Chapter 15: File I/O functions

Chapter 16: Exceptions Handling

Chapter 17: Classes and Objects

Chapter 18: Conclusion.

Chapter 1

Introduction to Python Programming Language

Did you know websites like YouTube and Dropbox use Python in their source code? Python is a vast language which is easy to understand and apply. You can develop almost anything using Python. Most of the operating systems (Mac, Linux, UNIX, etc.) other than windows have python installed by default. It is an open source and free language. In this eBook, we are going to learn this awesome code language and apply it on various examples. There are no type declaration of methods, parameters, functions or variables (like in other languages) in Python which makes its code short and simple. As mentioned earlier, this language can be used in everything, whether you want to build a website, a game or a search engine. The main advantage of using Python is that you do not have to run compiler explicitly, it is purely interpreted language like Perl or Shell.

File extension which is used by Python source file is ".py" and it is a case-sensitive language, so "P" and "p" would be considered as two different variables. Also, Python figures out the variable type on its own, for example, if you put x=4 and y='Python' then it will consider x as integer and y as string. We are going to learn all these basics in detail in further chapters. Before moving forward, few important points to remember are:

1. For assigning a value "=" is used and for comparison "==" is used. Example, x=4, y=8, x==y

2. "print" is used to print results.

3. All the mathematical operations like +, -, *, /, % are used with numbers

4. Variable is created when a value is assigned to it. Example, a=5 will create a variable named "a" which has an integer value of 5. There is no need to define it beforehand.

5. "+" can also be used to concatenate two string. Example, z= "Hi", z= z + "Python"

6.For logical operations "and", "or", "not" are used instead of symbols.

There are three basic data types: integer (by default for numbers), floats (a=3.125) and string. String can be defined either by "" (double quotes) or single quotes (''). We are going to see all the datatypes with proper examples in upcoming chapters.

Let's look at the step by step guide to install Python on Windows operating system. As mentioned earlier, if you are using other operating system like UNIX or Linux or Mac then Python should be installed already and ready to use. You have to use "%python" to get the details on Linux, press "CTRL + D" to exit. For running it on UNIX, "%python filename.py" is used. Python prompts with three "greater than" symbol (>>>).

Chapter 2

Installation and Environment Setup

In this chapter, we are going to see step by step guide to download and install Python language interpreter. After installation of the interpreter, we will integrate and set up Python development environment with eclipse IDE.

Python programming language is available for all of the three known platforms for Windows, Linux/Unix and Mac OS. Below are the links from where Python interpreters can be downloaded for these environments.

Windows platform

Python interpreter can be downloaded for windows platform using below link.

https://www.python.org/downloads/windows/

Options available on Python website are as follows:

Python 3.4.4 - 2015-12-21

- *Download Windows x86 MSI installer*

- *Download Windows x86-64 MSI installer*

- *Download Windows help file*

- *Download Windows debug information files for 64-bit binaries*

- *Download Windows debug information files*

In this tutorial, we are going to use windows platform to install Python 3.4.4 along with eclipse IDE to set up development environment.

LINUX/UNIX platform

If you are not able to find Python on your Linux or Unix OS then Python interpreter can be downloaded for LINUX or UNIX platform from below link.

https://www.python.org/downloads/

Different Linux version uses different package managers for installation of new packages. For example on Ubuntu, Python can be installed using the below command from terminal.

> *$sudo apt-get install python3-minimal*

It be installed from source using the below command.

Download Gzipped source tarball from Python's download URL : https://www.python.org/ftp/python/3.5.1/Python-3.5.1.tgz
Extract the tarball
tar xvfz Python-3.5.1.tgz
Configure and Install:
cd Python-3.5.1
./configure --prefix=/opt/python3.5.1

```
make
```

```
sudo make install
```

Mac OS Platform

Python interpreter can be downloaded for Mac OS platform from below link.

https://www.python.org/downloads/mac-osx/

Options available on Python website are as follows.

Python 3.4.4 - 2015-12-21

- *Download Mac OS X 64-bit/32-bit installer*

- *Download Mac OS X 32-bit i386/PPC installer*

Steps to install Python on Windows Platform

Please follow the below steps:

1. Check for Windows installer if it is 32-bit or 64-bit. Accordingly download Python version for Windows platform for the given link.

2. Once downloaded, click on the installer. Below screen will be visible which will trigger Python installation on Windows.

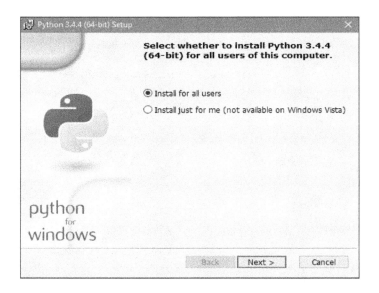

3. Choose the first option as "Install for all users" and click on the next button to proceed.

4. Next, system will ask to select destination directory. Choose the directory as shown below and click on Next button.

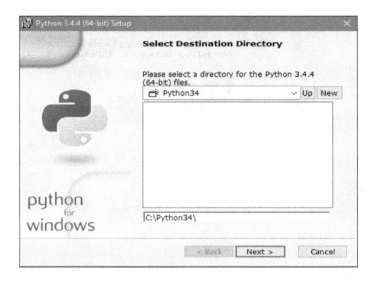

5. Next, system will ask to customize Python 3.4.4. Keep the default setup and click on the Next button as shown in the below screenshot.

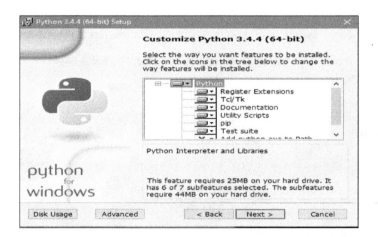

6. Installer will start the installation which will take several minutes and below screenshot will be visible during this point of time.

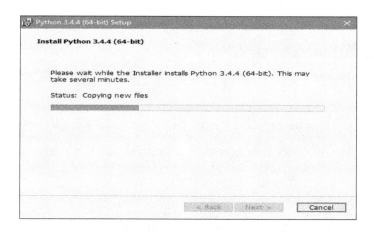

7. Once Python interpreter installation is completed, click on the finish button to complete the installation on Windows platform.

Steps to set up Python development environment on Eclipse IDE

Please follow the below steps:

1. Download the eclipse from below link. Choose the latest stable version of the eclipse and make sure that if your machine is 64-bit then chose 64-bit eclipse. In this tutorial, eclipse MARS.1 version is used.

https://eclipse.org/downloads

2. Click on the elipse.exe to open the eclipse which will ask to choose a local directory as its workspace as shown in the below screenshot.

3. Choose or create a directory on any available drive and click on the OK button to start eclipse.

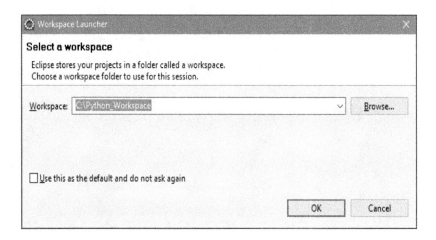

4. On the eclipse navigate as Help -> Install New software…

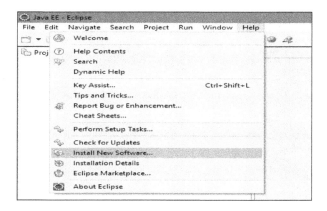

5. It will open a dialogue box in eclipse as shown in the below screenshot. In the textbox "work with:" enter the URL as http://pydev.org/updates and click on the add button. Next select the checkbox as "PyDev" and click on the Next button.

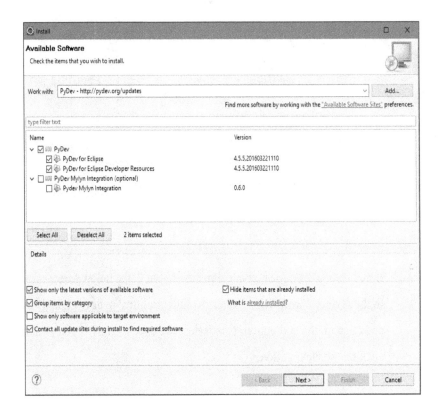

6. Next, system will ask to read and accept or decline the licence agreement. Accept the licence agreement in order to proceed the current software installation and click on the finish button as shown in the below screenshot.

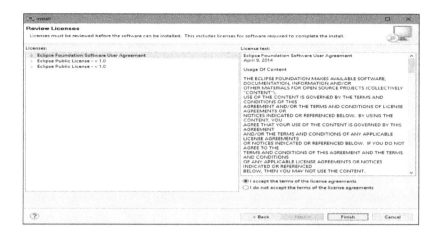

7. Above step will complete the installation of PyDev software on the eclipse. After installation it will prompt to restart eclipse. Upon eclipse restart, the Python development environment is ready to use on eclipse.

First Python project on eclipse

Please follow below steps.

1. Left handside of eclipse has Project Explorer. Right click in that region or navigate as New -> Project. Select PyDev from the Wizard as shown in the below screenshot.

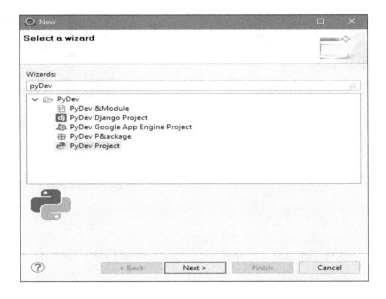

2. Select PyDev Project option from Wizard and click on next button to proceed.

3. It will open a PyDev project dialouge box asking for Project name, project type, grammer version and interpreter configuration.

4. Give the project name as "MyFirstPythonProject", project type as Python, and grammer version as 3.0-3.5.

5. Click on the given link to configure the Python interpreter as shown below. Here we just need to give the path of python.exe where we installed Python on C drive.

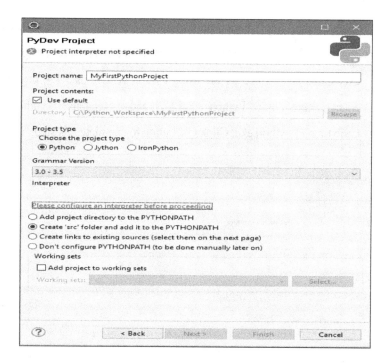

6. Click on the Interpreter link, it will ask for how to configure the interpreter, since we know Python installation path therfore select "Manual Config" option.

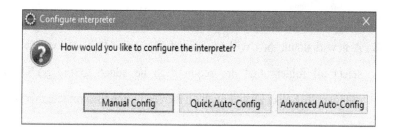

7. Click on the "New" button present at the top right corner and in the opened dialogue box enter the interpreter name and the interpreter executable path. Since we are using Python version as 3.4.4, therfore enter name as "Python 3.4.4" and executable path as C:\Python34\python.exe. Click OK button to complete this step.

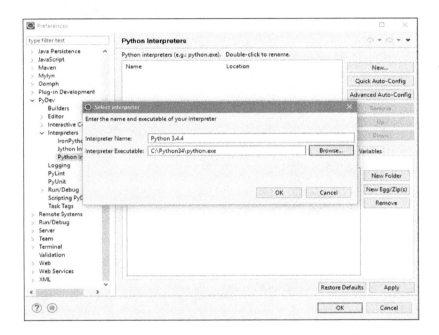

8. A new dialogue box will be opened as shown. This step will ask to select all folders that are required to be added to the SYSTEM pythonpath. Select all and click on the OK button to complete this step.

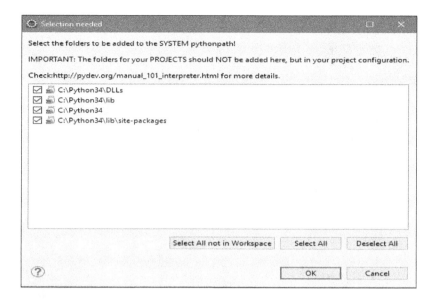

9. Next click on the Apply button and then OK button to complete the set up for Python first project as shown in the below screenshot.

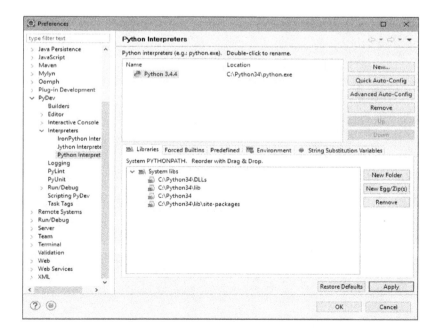

10. Lastly, click on the finish button to complete first "PyDev Project" set up in eclipse as shown in the below screenshot.

11. By this step, Python first project directory structure and path set up are ready as shown in the below screenshot.

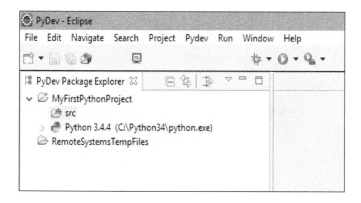

12. At the source directory, right click and navigate as New -> PyDev Module.

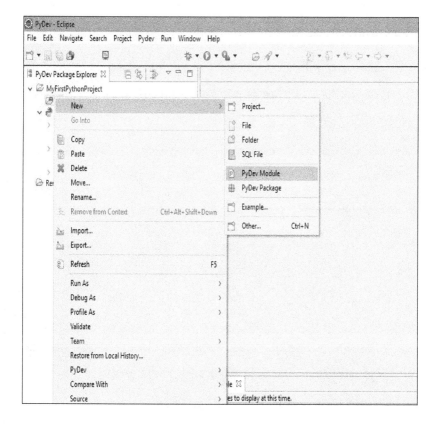

13. This will open a dialogue box asking to enter package and PyDev module name. Enter name as "FirstPython" and click on the finish button to complete this step as shown in the below screenshot.

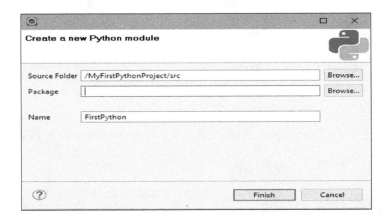

14. Above step will open up another dialogue box asking you to select the template for the Python project. Choose here <Empty> and click on the OK button.

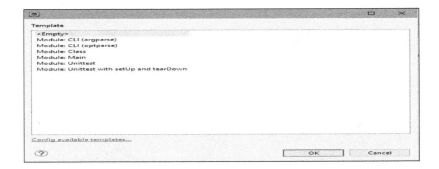

15. This will open the FirstPython.py file where we can edit and write the Python program code as shown in the below screenshot. Python program files has extension as .py.

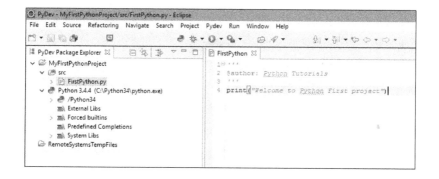

16. To run above Python program press Ctrl+F11 keys, it will open up below dialogue box. Select "Python Run" option and click OK button to complete this step.

17. Final output will be displayed at the bottom of the eclipse in console as shown in the below screenshot.

```
Console ⊠                                          ▣ ✖ ✖ ℚ 🖥
<terminated> C:\Python_Workspace\MyFirstPythonProject\src\FirstPython.py
Welcome to Python First project
```

This completes the installation, environment set up and execution for first Python program. In the next chapter, we are going to learn about various syntax used in Python programming.

Chapter 3
Syntax Used in Python

Python Identifiers

An identifier in any programming language is the name given to identify a variable, function, class, module or other object. In python language, an identifiers begins with an alphabetic letter A to Z or a to z or an underscore (_) followed by zero or more alphabetic letters, underscores and digits (0 to 9).

Python programming language does not allow special characters such as @, $, /, and % within identifiers. Python is a case sensitive programming language, therefore identifiers such as 'Python' and 'python' are two different identifiers in Python programming language.

Below are the naming conventions for identifiers in Python.

- Class name in python always begins with an uppercase letter and all other Python identifiers starts with a lowercase letter.

- A Python identifier is private when such identifier begins with a single leading underscore.

- A Python identifier is strongly private when such identifier begins with two leading underscores.

- A Python identifier is a language-defined special name when such identifier ends with two trailing underscores.

Python Reserve Words

Reserve words in any programming language are special commands that compiler or interpreters understands and these reserve words cannot be used as constant or variable or any other identifier names in that programming language.

Python has following reserve words and all such keywords contain lowercase letters only.

and	def	exec	if	not	return
assert	del	finally	import	or	try
break	elif	for	in	pass	while
class	else	from	is	print	with
continue	except	global	lambda	raise	yield

Python Keywords

Lines and Indentations

Any block of code in Python are denoted by line indentation, which is rigidly enforced. Python has no braces to denote blocks of code for class definitions and function definitions or flow control. The number of spaces used in an indentation can be variable but for all statements in a particular block, the number of spaces should always be same. For Example, below, block is correctly indented therefore there is no error.

```
P Demo ✕
1  if False:
2      print ("All is good")
3  else:
4      print ("All is bad")
5
6
```

In the next example, since the last statement in the block is not properly indented, therefore the block has an error.

```
P Demo ✕
1  if False:
2      print ("All is good")
3      print ("Python the best")
4  else:
5      print ("All is bad")
6          print ("Incorrect Indentations")
7
8
```

Therefore, conclusion is that, in Python programming language all the continuous lines indented with same number of spaces would form a block.

Representing a Statement as Multi-Line

Statements in Python language ends with a new line. If statement is required to be continued into the next line then line continuation character (\) is used in Python language. This line continuation character (\) denotes that the statement line should continue as shown in the below screenshot. In the below example, we have three variables result1, result2 and result3 and the final output is copied to the variable named result. Instead of writing the equation statement in a single line (result=result1+result2+result3), here, we have used line continuation character (\) so that, it could be written in three lines but represents a single statement in Python language.

```
Demo ⊠
 1  result1 = 7
 2  result2 = 9
 3  result3 = 90
 4
 5  result = result1 + \
 6              result2 + \
 7              result3
 8
 9  print("Result is: ")
10  print(result)
```

```
Console ⊠
<terminated> C:\Python_Workspace\MyFirstPythonProject\src\Demo.py
Result is:
106
```

Also, a Python statement which is defined within braces (), {} and [] does not require line continuation character (\) when written as multi-line statement. These kind of Python statements are still interpreted as single statement without use of line continuation character (\).

```
Demo    MultiLine ⊠
1  days = {"Monday","Tuesday",
2          "Wednesday","Thursday",
3          "Friday","Saturday",
4          "Sunday"}
5  print(days)
6  
7
```

```
Console ⊠
<terminated> C:\Python_Workspace\MyFirstPythonProject\src\MultiLine.py
{'Thursday', 'Tuesday', 'Saturday', 'Wednesday', 'Monday', 'Sunday', 'Friday'}
```

Quotation in Python

Python language permits the use of single ('), double (") and triple (''' or """) codes to represent a string literal, making sure that the same type of quote begins and ends that string. In the below example, single, double and triple codes are used to represent a string in a word, sentence or paragraph. When we print these variable they print the string irrespective of single, double and triple codes used for representing string literal in Python language.

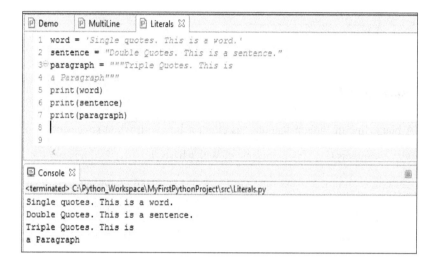

Comments in Python

Any comment in Python language is represented by a hash sign (#) provided it is not used inside a string literal between codes (single, double or triple). All characters after the hash sign (#) and up to the end of the physical line are the part of comment and Python interpreter ignores this statement while interpreting the whole program. In the below example, interpreter will just print the string present inside the print command and will ignore the parts mentioned after has sign before and after as comments.

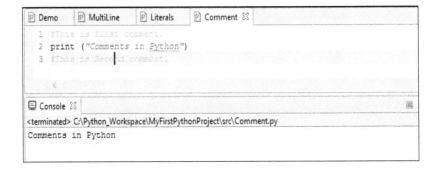

Using Blank Lines

A blank line in Python language is either a line with white spaces or a line with comments (i.e. statement starting with a hash sign (#)). Python interpreter while interpreting a blank line ignores it and no machine readable code will be generated. A multiline statement in Python is terminated after entering an empty physical line.

Waiting for the User

Using Python programming language, we can set up the prompt which can accept user's input. The following line of the program will display a prompt, which says "Press any key to exit", and waits for the user input or action.

```
#! /usr/bin/python

raw_input ("\n\nPress any key to exit.")
```

Also, in the above statement we have used "\n\n". This is used to create two new lines before displaying the actual line. Once the key is pressed by user, the program will end. By doing this we can keep a window console open until the user has finished his work with an application.

Multiple Statements on a Single Line

Python language allows to write multiple statements on a single line if they are separated by a semicolon (;) as demonstrated in the example below.

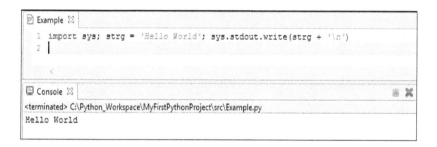

Multiple Statement Groups as Suites and Header Line

In Python language, a group of individual statements making a single code block are called suites. Whereas the compound or complex statements, such as if, def, while, and class require a suite and a header line.

Header line is the one that begins a statement (with the keyword like if, elif, else, etc.) and ends with a colon (:) and is followed by one or more lines which makes up the suite as demonstrated in the below example. Here, *if*

strg=='Hello World': is a header line which is followed by a suite (suite = 'Found').

```
Example ⌘
  1  import sys; strg = 'Hello World';
  2  if strg =='Hello World' :
  3     suite ='Found'
  4  elif strg =='Hello Python' :
  5     suite ='Very Close'
  6  else :
  7     suite ='Not Found'
  8  sys.stdout.write(suite + '\n')

Console ⌘                                                    ☐ ✖
<terminated> C:\Python_Workspace\MyFirstPythonProject\src\Example.py
Found
```

Command Line Arguments

On UNIX OS which has Python interpreter installed, we can take help and see all the lists of the functions. These are the basic ones. Below screenshot demonstrate the help command on UNIX system and all the functions or short codes used.

$ python -h

usage: python [option] ... [-c cmd | -m mod | file | -] [arg] ...

Options and arguments (and corresponding environment variables):

-c cmd: program passed in as string (terminates option list)

-d   : debug output from parser (also PYTHONDEBUG=x)

-E   : ignore environment variables (such as PYTHONPATH)

-h   : print this help message and exit

[etc.]

Chapter 4

Variable Types

Variables in any programming language are the names of the reference to the reserved memory locations which are used to store values. Similarly, when we are creating a variable in Python then we are reserving some space in the memory.

These variables have their own data type, based on the type, the interpreter allocates memory and decides what kind of data can be stored in these reserved memory locations. Characters, integers, decimals, etc. are the different data types which can be assigned to such variables.

Assigning Values to Variables

In Python language, equal sign (=) is used to assign values to the variables. Such variables do not need explicit declaration. When we assign a value to a variable, the declaration or creation happens automatically.

The operand to the left of the equal sign (=) is the name of the variable and the operand to the right of the equal sign (=) is the value stored in the variable. This is demonstrated in the below example.

```
P Variables ⊠
  1  number  = 100        # An integer value
  2  decimal = 10000.0    # A floating value
  3  name    = "Martin"   # A string
  4
  5  print (number)
  6  print (decimal)
  7  print (name)
  8
     <

🖥 Console ⊠                                                              ▣ ✖
<terminated> C:\Python_Workspace\MyFirstPythonProject\src\Variables.py
100
10000.0
Martin
```

In the above example, variable name 'number' has an integer value therefore it behave as an integer without any data type declaration. Similarly, variable name 'decimal' has a floating value and variable name 'name' has a string value. Python is very flexible language since it automatically determines the data type once the value is assigned to the variable.

Multiple Assignment

Python language allows assignment of a single value to more than one variables and multiple values to multiple variables which are separated by commas in a single line as demonstrated in the below example.

```
P MultiAssignment ⊠
1  a=b=c=d= 1000
2
3  k,l,m =  "Jose","Patrick","Peter"
4
5  print(l)
6  print(b)
  -
     <
```

```
🖳 Console ⊠                                                          🖺 ✖
<terminated> C:\Python_Workspace\MyFirstPythonProject\src\MultiAssignment.py
Patrick
1000
```

In the first case (many-t0-one), single value 1000 is assigned to many variables a, b, c and d.

In the second case (many-to-many), multiple values ("Jose", "Patrick", "Peter") are assigned to multiple variables k, l and m. However, here is one to one mapping between a variable and a value, e.g. variable k will contain value as "Jose", variable l will contain value as "Patrick" and variable m will contain value as "Peter".

Standard Data Types in Python

In Python, the data is stored in memory which can be of many types. For example, a person's birth year is stored as a numeric value and his or her qualifications are stored as alphanumeric characters. Depending on the type of value, the Python has different standard data types that are used to define the type of value a variable can contain.

Python language has five standard data types. We are going to discuss them in detail. These are:

➢ Numbers

- ➢ Strings

- ➢ Lists

- ➢ Tuples

- ➢ Dictionary

Python Numbers

In Python language, the number data type are used to store numeric values. Numeric variable are created automatically in Python when we assign a numeric value to it as shown in the below example.

```
Number 

1  variable1 = 198
2  variable2 = 12.87
3
4  print(variable1)
5  print(variable2)

Console 
<terminated> C:\Python_Workspace\MyFirstPythonProject\src\Number.py
198
12.87
```

Python supports below four different numerical types.

- ➢ int (signed integers)

- ➢ long (long integers, they can also be represented in hexadecimal and octal)

- ➢ float (floating point real values)

> complex (complex numbers)

Below are the examples of number objects in Python language.

Int	Long	float	Complex
40	7965391L	0.0	8.14j
900	-0x29546L	17.90	675.j
-589	0455L	-31.9	23.8922e-36j
050	0xABDDAECCBEABCBFE ACl	62.3+e68	.6776j
-0630	563213626792L	-560.	-.6844+0J
- 0x1290	-032318432823L	-82.53e200	4e+86J
0x37	-5627995245529L	40.2-E52	7.59e-7j

Below are few things to note about Python number objects.

> A complex number consists of an ordered pair of real floating-point numbers denoted by (real + img**j**), where real and img are the real numbers and j is the imaginary number unit.

> Python displays long integers (data type number) with an uppercase L.

> Python language allows to use a lowercase L with long data type number, however it is recommended to use only an uppercase L in order to avoid confusion with the number 1.

In Python, we can delete the reference to a number object (variable) by using the 'del' statement. Given below is the syntax of the 'del' statement.

```
del
variable1[,variable2[,variable3[....,variableN]]]]
```

Using the above statement, we can delete a single variable or multiple variables by using the 'del' statement as shown in the below example.

```
Number ⊠
 1  variable1 = 198
 2  variable2 = 12.87
 3  variable3 = 32.87
 4  variable4 = 52.87
 5
 6  del variable1
 7  del variable2,variable3
 8
 9  print(variable2)
10  print(variable4)
```

```
Console ⊠
<terminated> C:\Python_Workspace\MyFirstPythonProject\src\Number.py
Traceback (most recent call last):
  File "C:\Python Workspace\MyFirstPythonProject\src\Number.py", line 9, in <module>
    print(variable2)
NameError: name 'variable2' is not defined
```

In the above example, since we have deleted variable2 using the 'del' command, this variable do not exist anymore when we tried to print it.

Strings in Python

In Python language, Strings are identified as a contiguous set of characters which are represented within the quotation marks. Python language permits the use of single ('), double (") and triple (''' or """) codes to represent a string literal, making sure that the same type of quote begins and ends that string.

Strings in Python have below operators.

➤ **Slice operator ([ ] and [:]).** By using the slice operator ([ ] and [:]) with indexes starting at 0 in the beginning of the string and working their way from -1 at the end, subsets of strings can be taken.

➤ **Plus (+) sign operator.** By using the plus (+) sign operator, we can concatenate two or more strings.

➤ **Asterisk (*) sign operator.** Asterisk operator is the repetition operator. If we want to print string 3 times then simply we can give command as print (string * 3).

All of above operators are demonstrated in the below example.

```python
strg = 'Hello Python!'

print (strg)                        # Prints the complete string
print (strg[3])                     # Prints third character of the string
print (strg[1:8])                   # Prints characters starting from 1st to 8th
print (strg[3:])                    # Prints string starting from 4th character
print (strg * 3)                    # Prints string three times
print (strg + "Concatenate Demo")   # Prints concatenated string
```

```
Console ☒
<terminated> C:\Python_Workspace\MyFirstPythonProject\src\String.py
Hello Python!
1
ello Py
lo Python!
Hello Python!Hello Python!Hello Python!
Hello Python!Concatenate Demo
```

Lists in Python

In Python language, a List is the most versatile compound data types. A list contains items which are separated by commas and enclosed within square brackets ([]). Lists are similar to arrays in C or C++ in some extents. The difference between arrays in C /C++ and lists in Python is that the former cannot have different datatype for elements while latter can have different datatype for elements.

```
1  listsdemo = ( 'xyz', 543 , 9.43, 'peter', 670.2  )
2  smalllists = (543, 'patrick')
3
4  print (listsdemo)                    # Prints the complete list
5  print (listsdemo[1])                 # Prints second element of the list
6  print (listsdemo[1:2])               # Prints elements starting from 1st till 2nd
7  print (listsdemo[3:])                # Prints elements starting from 4th element
8  print (smalllists * 2)               # Prints list two times
9  print (listsdemo + smalllists)       # Prints concatenated lists
```

```
Console X
<terminated> C:\Python_Workspace\MyFirstPythonProject\src\Lists.py
('xyz', 543, 9.43, 'peter', 670.2)
543
(543,)
('peter', 670.2)
(543, 'patrick', 543, 'patrick')
('xyz', 543, 9.43, 'peter', 670.2, 543, 'patrick')
```

Lists in Python have below operators.

> **Slice operator ([ ] and [:]).** By using the slice operator ([ ] and [:]) with element position starting at 0 in the beginning of the list and working their way from -1 at the end, subsets of the list can be taken.

- ➢ **Plus (+) sign operator.** By using the plus (+) sign operator, we can concatenate two or more lists.

- ➢ **Asterisk (*) sign operator**. Asterisk operator is the repetition operator. If we want to print a list 2 times then simply we can give command as print (listsdemo * 2).

Tuples in Python

In Python language, a tuple is a sequence data type which is almost similar to the list. A tuple consists of a number of values which are comma separated. Unlike lists, tuples are enclosed within parentheses.

The main differences between tuples and lists are as follows.

- ➢ Tuples are enclosed in parentheses (( )) whereas Lists are enclosed in brackets ([ ]).

- ➢ Tuples are read-only lists as their elements and size cannot be changed, while Lists can be updated. We can change lists elements and size.

```
Tuples ⊠
1  tuplesdemo = ( 'xyz', 543 , 9.43, 'peter', 670.2  )
2  smalltuples = (543, 'patrick')
3
4  print (tuplesdemo)                    # Prints complete list
5  print (tuplesdemo[1])                 # Prints second element of the list
6  print (tuplesdemo[2:4])               # Prints elements starting from 3rd till 4th
7  print (tuplesdemo[1:])                # Prints elements starting from 1st element
8  print (tuplesdemo * 2)                # Prints list two times
9  print (tuplesdemo + smalltuples)      # Prints concatenated lists
```

```
Console ⊠
<terminated> C:\Python_Workspace\MyFirstPythonProject\src\Tuples.py
('xyz', 543, 9.43, 'peter', 670.2)
543
(9.43, 'peter')
(543, 9.43, 'peter', 670.2)
('xyz', 543, 9.43, 'peter', 670.2, 'xyz', 543, 9.43, 'peter', 670.2)
('xyz', 543, 9.43, 'peter', 670.2, 543, 'patrick')
```

Tuples in Python have below operators.

> **Slice operator ([ ] and [:]).** By using the slice operator ([ ] and [:]) with element position starting at 0 in the beginning of the tuple and working their way from -1 at the end, subsets of the tuple can be taken.

> **Plus (+) sign operator.** By using the plus (+) sign operator, we can concatenate two or more tuples.

> **Asterisk (*) sign operator.** Asterisk operator is the repetition operator. If we want to print a tuple 2 times then simply we can give command as print (tuplesdemo * 2).

Dictionary in Python

A dictionary in Python represents hash table. A hash table (or hash map) is a data structure which is used to implement an associative array, a structure that can map keys to values. To compute an index of an array of buckets or slots, a hash table uses a hash function to procure the desired value. This concept in Python work like associative arrays or hashes found in Perl and consist of key-value pairs. Keys in Python dictionary can be of any data type, however mostly they are either numbers or strings. On the other hand, values in Python dictionary are Python objects.

In Python, syntax wise there are two ways dictionaries can be created which are mentioned below:

1. Dictionary name is given with curly braces ({ }) first (E.g. veggie = {}). Next we can define the key value pairs one by one as (E.g. veggie ["tomatoes"] = 20). Here, key is tomatoes and the value is 20.

2. Dictionary can also be defined with all key value pairs in one go within the curly braces ({}). (E.g. fruits = {'apple': 'Good','banana':'Better', 'orange': 'Best'}). Here, dictionary name is 'fruits', 'apple' is one of the key of such dictionary and 'Good' is the associated value with this key.

These syntaxes are demonstrated in the below example.

```
dictionary ⊠
1  veggie = {}
2  # Add three key-value tuples to the dictionary.
3  veggie["tomatoes"] = 20
4  veggie["potato"] = 46
5  veggie["onions"] = 47
6  fruits = {'apple': 'Good','banana':'Better', 'orange': 'Best'}
7  # Get syntax 1.
8  print(veggie["tomatoes"])
9
10 # Get syntax 2.
11 print(veggie.get("carrot"))
12 print(veggie.get("carrot", "no tuna found"))
13 print(fruits)
```

```
Console ⊠                                                              🗎 ✖
<terminated> C:\Python_Workspace\MyFirstPythonProject\src\dictionary.py
20
None
no tuna found
{'apple': 'Good', 'banana': 'Better', 'orange': 'Best'}
```

Data Type Conversion

While writing programming code, we may need to perform data type conversions. To support such operations, Python language has several built-in functions which are used to perform conversion from one data type to another. After conversion, these functions return a new object representing the converted value. Below is the list of Python built-in functions along with their operational description.

Function	Description
int(value [,Base])	This function converts value into an integer. "Base" specifies the base if value is a string.

long(value [,Base])	This function converts value into a long integer. "Base" specifies the base if value is a string.
chr(value)	This function converts an integer into a character.
complex(real [,imag])	This function is used to create a complex number.
dict(Value)	This function is used to create a dictionary. "Value" must be a sequence of (key, value) tuples.
eval(strg)	This function is used to evaluate a string which returns an object.
float(value)	This function converts value into a floating-point number.
frozenset(value)	This function converts value into a frozen set.
hex(value)	This function converts an integer value into a hexadecimal string.
list(value)	This function converts value to a list.
repr(value)	This function is used to convert an object value to an expression string.
oct(value)	This function is used to converts an integer value to an octal string.
ord(value)	This function is used to converts a single character to its integer value.
set(value)	This function is used to convert value into a set.

str(value)	This function is used to convert an object value into a string representation.
tuple(value)	This function is used to convert value into a tuple.
unichr(value)	This function is used to convert an integer value into a Unicode character.

Chapter 5

Operators

Operators can be defined as the constructs which can manipulate the value of operands.

Consider the expression 9 - 4 = 5. Here, 9 and 4 are known as operands and - is known as operator.

Types of Operator

In Python language, following are the operators that are supported.

> Arithmetic Operators

> Assignment Operators

> Bitwise Operators

> Comparison (Relational) Operators

> Identity Operators

> Logical Operators

> Membership Operators

Let us have a look on all above Python operators one by one.

Arithmetic Operators in Python

Assume variable x holds 30 and variable y holds 30, then −

Operator	Description	Example
(+) Addition	It is a binary operator that adds values on either side of the operator.	x + y = 60
(-) Subtraction	It is a binary operator that subtracts right hand operand from left hand operand.	x − y = 0
(*) Multiplication	It is a binary operator that multiplies values on either side of the operator.	x * y = 900
(/) Division	It is a binary operator that divides left hand operand by right hand operand.	y / x = 1
(%) Modulus	It is a binary operator that divides left hand operand by right hand operand and returns remainder.	y % x = 0
(**) Exponent	It is a binary operator that performs exponential (power) calculation on operators.	x**y =30 to the power 30
(//) Floor Division	It is a floor Division operator. The division of operands where the result is the quotient and the digits after the decimal point are	7//2 = 3 and 5.0//2.0 = 2.0, -11//3 = -4, -11.0//3 = -4.0

| | removed. But in the case of the operands which are negative, the result is floored and rounded away from zero (towards negative infinity). | |

Assignment Operators in Python

In the below example, let us assume variable x holds a value of 10 and variable y holds a value of 20. Variable z is the result operand.

Operator	Description	Example
=	It assigns values from right side operands to left side operand.	z = x + y assigns value of x + y into z which is equal to 30.
+= Add AND	It adds the value of right operand to the value of the left operand and assign the result to left operand.	z += x is equivalent to z = z+ x.
-= Subtract AND	It subtracts the value of right operand from the value of left operand and assign the result to left operand.	z -= x is equivalent to z = z – x.
*= Multiply AND	It multiplies the value of right operand with the value of left	z *= x is equivalent to z = z * x.

	operand and assign the result to left operand.	
/= Divide AND	It divides the value of left operand with the value of right operand and assign the result to left operand.	z /= x is equivalent to z = z / x.
%=Modulus AND	It takes modulus on the values using two operands and assign the result to left operand.	z %= x is equivalent to z = z % x.
**=Exponent AND	It performs exponential (power) calculation on the operators and assigns the result to the left operand.	z **= x is equivalent to z = z ** x.
//= Floor Division	It performs floor division on the operators and assigns the result to the left operand.	z //= x is equivalent to z= z // x.

Bitwise Operators in Python

Bitwise operator are operators that work on the bits and performs bit by bit operation. For example, if variable x = 60; and variable y = 13; then their equivalent binary format will be as follows.

x = 0011 1100; y = 0000 1101. In the below example, binary AND, OR, XOR and Ones complement operations are demonstrated using Python bitwise operators.

```
Bitwiseoperator ⊠

 1  x = 60
 2  y = 13
 3
 4  print (x&y)    # Binary AND Operator
 5  print (x|y)    # Binary OR Operator
 6  print (x^y)    # Binary XOR Operator
 7  print (~x)     # Binary Ones Complement Operator
 8  print (x<<2)   # Binary Left Shift Operator
 9  print (x>>2)   # Binary Right Shift Operator
    <
```

```
Console ⊠                                                                ▣ ✖
<terminated> C:\Python_Workspace\MyFirstPythonProject\src\Bitwiseoperator.py
12
61
49
-61
240
15
```

Python language supports the following Bitwise operators.

Operator	Description	Example
& Binary AND	Binary AND operator copies a bit to the result if it is present in both operands.	(x & y) will give the result as 12. (0000 1100 in binary).
| Binary OR	Binary OR operator copies a bit if it is present in either operand.	(x | y) will give the result as 61. (0011 1101 in binary).
^ Binary XOR	Binary XOR operator copies the bit if it is set in one operand but not both.	(x ^ y) will give the result as 49. (0011 0001 in binary).

~ Binary Ones Complement	Binary Ones Complement operator is an unary and has the effect of 'flipping' bits.	(~x) will give the result as -61. (1100 0011 in binary). 2's complement form due to a signed binary number.
<< Binary Left Shift	In Binary Left Shift operator, the left operands value is moved left by the number of bits specified by the right operand.	x <<2 will give the result as 240 (1111 0000 in binary).
>> Binary Right Shift	In Binary Right Shift operator, the left operands value is moved right by the number of bits specified by the right operand.	x >>2 will give the result as 15 (0000 1111 in binary).

Comparison (Relational) Operators in Python

Comparison operators in Python language compare the values on either sides of them and decide whether the relation among them is true or false. They are also known as relational operators.

In the below example, variable x holds 20 and variable y holds 30.

Operator	Description	Example

==	For this relational operator, if the values of two operands are equal, then the condition becomes true.	(x == y) is false as both have different values.
!=	For this relational operator, if values of two operands are not equal, then condition becomes true.	(x != y) is true as both have different values
<>	For this relational operator, if values of two operands are not equal, then condition becomes true.	(x <> y) is true. This is similar to (!=) operator.
>	For this relational operator, if the value of left operand is greater than the value of right operand, then condition becomes true.	(x > y) is false as the value of x is less than the value of y.
<	For this relational operator, if the value of left operand is less than the value of right operand, then condition becomes true.	(x < y) is true as the value of x is less than the value of y.
>=	For this relational operator, if the value of left operand is greater than or equal to the value of right operand, then condition becomes true.	(x >= y) is false as the value of x is neither greater nor equal to the value of y.

<=	For this relational operator, if the value of left operand is less than or equal to the value of right operand, then condition becomes true.	(x <= y) is true as the value of x is less than the value of y. Although they are not equal yet the result is true as the first condition is true.

Identity Operators in Python

Python language has two identity operators (is and is not). Identity operators are operators that compare the memory locations of two objects. Both of the identity operators are explained below.

Operator	Description	Example
Is	This identity operator evaluates to true if the variables on either side of the operator point to the same object (memory location reference). Otherwise it evaluates to false.	x is y, in this case the results is 1 if ref(x) equals ref(y).
is not	This identity operator evaluates to false if the variables on either side of the operator point to the same object (memory location	x is not y, in this case the result is 1 if ref(x) is not equal to ref(y).

	reference). Otherwise it evaluates to true.	

Logical Operators in Python

Python supports three logical operators and, or and not. Following are their description with example.

Operator	Description	Example
and (Logical AND)	If both the operands are true then condition becomes true.	If x and y are true then the condition becomes true else false.
or (Logical OR)	If any of the two operands are non-zero then condition becomes true.	If x or y are true then the condition becomes true else false.
not (Logical NOT)	It is used to reverse the logical state of its operand.	If x is true then Not (x) will be false and vice-versa.

Membership Operators in Python

In Python language, the membership operators test for membership in a sequence, such as lists, tuples, or strings. Both of the membership operators are explained below.

Operator	Description	Example
In	This membership operator evaluates to true if it finds that a variable is the member in the specified sequence and otherwise it evaluates to false.	x in y, in this case the results is 1 if x is a member of sequence y.
not in	This membership operator evaluates to true if it does not finds a variable is the member in the specified sequence and otherwise it evaluates to false.	x not in y, in this the result is 1 if x is not a member of sequence y.

Operators Precedence in Python

Below table has a lists of all operators from highest precedence to lowest precedence in Python language.

Operator	Description
**	Exponentiation (raise to the power)
~ + -	Ones complement, unary plus and minus.

* / % //	Multiply, divide, modulo and floor division.
+ -	Addition and subtraction.
>> <<	Right and left bitwise shift.
&	Bitwise 'AND'.
^ |	Bitwise exclusive `OR' and regular `OR'.
<= < > >=	Comparison operators.
<> == !=	Equality operators.
= %= /= //= -= += *= **=	Assignment operators.
is, is not	Identity operators.
in, not in	Membership operators.
not, or, and	Logical operators.

Chapter 6

Loops

When any program is executed, it runs sequentially. The statement which appears first in the sequence is executed first then the next statement and so on till the last statement of the program. Many times there is a requirement to run same block of code in a program multiple times then there arise a need of a control structure known as loops.

A loop makes a statement or group of statements in a block of code to execute multiple times if the condition is true and exits the loop when the condition becomes false. Such loop is illustrated in the below diagram.

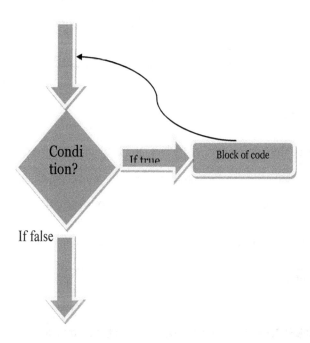

Types of Loop in Python

In Python programming language, following are the types of loops used to handle looping requirements.

Loop Type	Description
while loop	While loop type, repeats a statement or group of statements while a given condition is true. It tests the condition each time it executes the loop body and it exits the loop when condition becomes false.
for loop	For loop type executes a sequence of statements multiple times and abbreviates the code that manages the loop variable.
nested loops	It is a loop within a loop. In Python we can use a while loop in another while or for loop or for loop in another while or for loop.

Loop Control Statements in Python

Loop control statements in Python are used to change execution from its normal sequence. When such execution leaves a scope, all automatic objects that were created in that scope are destroyed or removed.

In Python language, the following control statements are supported.

Control Statement	Description
break statement	The break statement in Python is used to terminate the loop statement and transfers execution to the

	statement immediately following after the end of loop.
continue statement	The continue statement in Python is used to cause the loop to skip the remainder of its body and immediately retest its condition prior to reiterating the looping body.
pass statement	The pass statement in Python is used when a statement is required syntactically but we do not want any command or code to execute on that statement.

Loop and Control Statement Python Code Example

While Statement

The syntax of a while loop in Python programming language is as follows.

```
while expression:

statement(s)
```

Example code for while loop in Python.

```
P while ⊠
1  count = 0
2  while (count < 3):
3      print ('The current count is:', count)
4      count = count + 1
5
6  print ("While Loop Ended!")
7
```

```
Console ⊠                                                          ▣ ✖
<terminated> C:\Python_Workspace\MyFirstPythonProject\src\while.py
The current count is: 0
The current count is: 1
The current count is: 2
While Loop Ended!
```

For Statement

The syntax of a 'for' loop in Python programming language is as follows.

> *for iterating_var in sequence:*
>
> *statements (s)*

Example code for 'for' loop in Python.

```
P forloop ⊠
1  veggies = ['potato', 'tomatoes', 'onion']
2  for index in range(len(veggies)):
3      print ('The Current Veggie :', veggies[index])
4
5  print ("For loop ended!")
```

```
Console ⊠                                                          ▣ ✖
<terminated> C:\Python_Workspace\MyFirstPythonProject\src\forloop.py
The Current Veggie : potato
The Current Veggie : tomatoes
The Current Veggie : onion
For loop ended!
```

Nested Loop

As explained earlier, it is a loop within a loop. Below is the syntax for nested for loop in Python.

```
for iterating_var in sequence:

    for iterating_var in sequence:

        statements(s)

    statements(s)
```

Below is the syntax for nested while loop in Python.

```
while expression:

    while expression:

        statement(s)

    statement(s)
```

Below is an example for 'while nested loop in Python along with it's output.

```
P whilenestedloop ⨉
1  count1 = 0
2  while(count1 < 3):
3      count2 = 0
4      while(count2 < 3):
5          print ("Current values for count1 is ", count1, "and count2 is ", count2)
6          count2 = count2 + 1
7      count1 = count1 + 1
8
9  print ("Exiting Nested While Loop!")
```

```
Console ⨉                                                              ▣ ✖ ✕ Q
<terminated> C:\Python_Workspace\MyFirstPythonProject\src\whilenestedloop.py
Current values for count1 is  0 and count2 is  0
Current values for count1 is  0 and count2 is  1
Current values for count1 is  0 and count2 is  2
Current values for count1 is  1 and count2 is  0
Current values for count1 is  1 and count2 is  1
Current values for count1 is  1 and count2 is  2
Current values for count1 is  2 and count2 is  0
Current values for count1 is  2 and count2 is  1
Current values for count1 is  2 and count2 is  2
Exiting Nested While Loop!
```

Example on control statements in Python

```
P controlstatement ✕
 1  count1=count2=0
 2  print("First example on break statement")
 3  while (count1 < 4):              # First Example
 4      print ("for loop Processing current count1: ", count1)
 5      if (count1==1):
 6          break
 7          print ("Break not happened on count1: ", count1)
 8      count1=count1 + 1
 9  print ("Break  happened on count1: ", count1)
10  print("second example on continue statement")
11  while (count2 < 2):              # First Example
12      print ("for loop Processing current count2: ", count2)
13      if (count2==2):
14          count2=count2 + 1
15          continue
16          print ("Continue happened on count2: ", count2)
17      else:
18          print ("Continue not happened on count2: ", count2)
19      count2=count2 + 1
20  print ("Exit  happened on count2: ", count2)
```

Console ✕   ▣ ✕

```
<terminated> C:\Python_Workspace\MyFirstPythonProject\src\controlstatement.py
First example on break statement
for loop Processing current count1:  0
for loop Processing current count1:  1
Break  happened on count1:  1
second example on continue statement
for loop Processing current count2:  0
Continue not happened on count2:  0
for loop Processing current count2:  1
Continue not happened on count2:  1
Exit  happened on count2:  2
```

Chapter 7

Decision Making

While writing a program, most of the time we face a situation where we have to make a decision. Decision making is anticipation of conditions that could occur while execution of a program and there is a need to specify some actions according to those conditions.

In a decision making structures, there is a condition which is either a single expression or multiple expressions. This condition when evaluated produce either TRUE or FALSE as outcome. Based on the outcome, we need to determine which action to take and which statements to execute. Refer the figure below to understand it clearly.

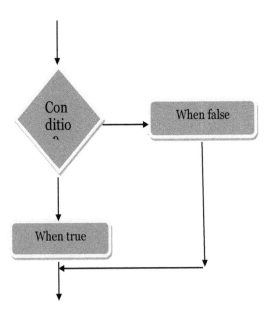

Above is the general form of a decision making structure that is found in most of the programming languages including Python.

In Python programming language, it should be noted that any non-zero and non-null values are assumed as TRUE, however if it is either zero or null, in that case it is assumed as FALSE value.

Following are the types of decision making statements in Python language.

Statement	Description
if statements	An 'if' statement consists of a boolean expression which generally follows either one or more statements.
if...else statements	An 'if' statement can be followed by an optional else statement. When the boolean expression is TRUE then the statements in 'if' block are executed and if it is FALSE then the statements in 'else' block are executed skipping the statements present in 'if' block.
Nested if...elif...else statements	Nested 'if' statements are 'if...elif...else' statements within other 'if' statement.

Syntax for if and if...else statement.

Below is the syntax for if statement alone in Python language.

if expression:

```
statement(s)
```

Below is the syntax for if...else statement alone in Python language.

```
if expression:

    statement (s)

else:

statement (s)
```

Python code example on if...else statement

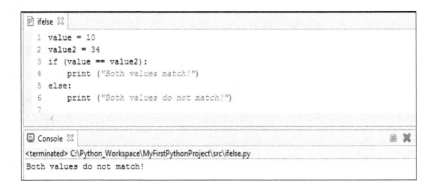

Python Code example to demonstrate Nested if-elif-else statement.

Below is the syntax of the nested if...elif...else construct may be:

```
if expression1:

    statement(s)

    if expression2:

        statement(s)

    elif expression3:

        statement(s)

    else

        statement(s)

elif expression4:

    statement(s)

else:

    statement(s)
```

```
P nestedifelse ⊠
  1  value = 10
  2  if value < 20:
🔎 3      print ("Logical expression value is less than 20")
  4      if value == 15:
  5          print ("Given value is 15")
  6      elif value == 10:
  7          print ("Given value is 10")
  8      elif value == 5:
  9          print ("Given value is 5")
 10  elif value < 5:
 11      print ("Logical Expression value is less than 5")
 12  else:
 13      print ("Could not find true expression")
 14
 15  print ("Demo for if...elif...else ends!")
         ‹
```

```
🖥 Console ⊠                                                           ▣  ✖  ✖
<terminated> C:\Python_Workspace\MyFirstPythonProject\src\nestedifelse.py
Logical expression value is less than 20
Given value is 10
Demo for if...elif...else ends!
```

Chapter 8

Python in-built Strings and Numbers Functions

In the previous chapters, we have already discussed about how to declare string and numbers in Python. In this chapter, we are going to discuss about various Python in-built mathematical, random number, trigonometric functions and their use on numbers and in-built string methods.

Mathematical functions

Function	Returns (description)
abs(x)	This function determines the absolute value of x, which is the (positive) distance between x and zero.
ceil(x)	This function determines the ceiling of x, which is the smallest integer not less than x.
cmp(x, y)	This function returns values as -1, 0 and 1. It returns-1 if x < y, 0 if x == y, or 1 if x > y.
exp(x)	This function determines the exponential of x: ex.
fabs(x)	This function determines the absolute value of x.
floor(x)	This function determines the floor of x, which is the largest integer not greater than x.
log(x)	This function determines the natural logarithm of x, for x> 0.

log10(x)	This function determines the base-10 logarithm of x for x> 0.
max (x1, x2,..)	This function determines the largest of its arguments, which is the value closest to positive infinity.
min (x1, x2,..)	This function determines the smallest of its arguments, which is the value closest to negative infinity
modf(x)	This function determines the fractional and integer parts of x in a two-item tuple. Both parts have the same sign as x. The integer part is returned as a float by the function.
pow(x, y)	This function determines the value of x**y.
round(x [,n])	In this function, x rounded to n digits from the decimal point. Python rounds away from zero as a tie-breaker, round (0.5) is 1.0 and round (-0.5) is -1.0.
sqrt(x)	This function determines the square root of x for x > 0.

Random Number functions

Function	Description
choice(seq)	This function returns a random item from a list, tuple, or string.
randrange ([start,] stop [,step])	This function returns a randomly selected element from range (start, stop, step).
random()	This function returns a random float r, such that 0 is less than or equal to r and r is less than 1.

seed([x])	This function sets the integer starting value used in generating random numbers. Call this function before calling any other random module function. Returns None.
shuffle(lst)	This function is used to randomize the items of a list in place. It returns Nothing.
uniform(x, y)	This function returns a random float r, such that x is less than or equal to r and r is less than y.

Trigonometric functions

Function	Description
acos(x)	This Python in-built trigonometric function returns the arc cosine of x, in radians.
asin(x)	This Python in-built trigonometric function returns the arc sine of x, in radians.
atan(x)	This Python in-built trigonometric function returns the arc tangent of x, in radians.
atan2(y, x)	This Python in-built trigonometric function returns atan(y / x), in radians.
cos(x)	This Python in-built trigonometric function returns the cosine of x radians.
hypot(x, y)	This Python in-built trigonometric function returns the Euclidean norm, sqrt(x*x + y*y).
sin(x)	This Python in-built trigonometric function returns the sine of x radians.

tan(x)	This Python in-built trigonometric function returns the tangent of x radians.
degrees(x)	This Python in-built trigonometric function converts angle x from radians to degrees.
radians(x)	This Python in-built trigonometric function converts angle x from degrees to radians.

Mathematical Constants

Constants	Description
Pi	The mathematical constant pi.
E	The mathematical constant e.

Python in-built String Methods

Methods	Description
capitalize()	This Python in-built function is for String which makes first letter of the string in uppercase
center(width, fillchar)	This Python in-built function for String returns a space-padded string with the original string centered to a total of width columns.
count(str, beg= 0,end=len(string))	This Python in-built function for String counts how many times str occurs in string or in a substring of string if starting index beg and ending index end are given.

decode(encoding='UTF-8',errors='strict')	This Python in-built function for String decodes the string using the codec registered for encoding. Encoding defaults to the default string encoding.
encode(encoding='UTF-8',errors='strict')	This Python in-built function for String returns encoded string version of string; on error, default is to raise a ValueError unless errors is given with 'ignore' or 'replace'.
endswith(suffix, beg=0, end=len(string))	This Python in-built function for String determines if string or a substring of string (if starting index beg and ending index end are given) ends with suffix; returns true if so and false otherwise.
expandtabs(tabsize=8)	This Python in-built function for String expands tabs in string to multiple spaces; defaults to 8 spaces per tab if tabsize not provided.
find(str, beg=0 end=len(string))	This Python in-built function for String determine if str occurs in string or in a substring of string if starting index beg and ending index end are given returns index if found and -1 otherwise.
index(str, beg=0, end=len(string))	This Python in-built function for String is same as find(), but raises an exception if str not found.
isalnum()	This Python in-built function for String returns true if string has at least 1 character and all characters are alphanumeric and false otherwise.

isalpha()	This Python in-built function for String returns true if string has at least 1 character and all characters are alphabetic and false otherwise.
isdigit()	This Python in-built function for String returns true if string contains only digits and false otherwise.
islower()	This Python in-built function for String returns true if string has at least 1 cased character and all cased characters are in lowercase and false otherwise.
isnumeric()	This Python in-built function for String returns true if a Unicode string contains only numeric characters and false otherwise.
isspace()	This Python in-built function for String returns true if string contains only whitespace characters and false otherwise.
istitle()	This Python in-built function for String returns true if string is properly "titlecased" and false otherwise.
isupper()	This Python in-built function for String returns true if string has at least one cased character and all cased characters are in uppercase and false otherwise.
join(seq)	This Python in-built function for String merges (concatenates) the string representations of

	elements in sequence seq into a string, with separator string.
len(string)	This Python in-built function for String returns the length of the string
ljust(width[, fillchar])	This Python in-built function for String returns a space-padded string with the original string left-justified to a total of width columns.
lower()	This Python in-built function for String converts all uppercase letters in string to lowercase.
lstrip()	This Python in-built function for String removes all leading whitespace in string.
maketrans()	This Python in-built function for String returns a translation table to be used in translate function.
max(str)	This Python in-built function for String returns the max alphabetical character from the string str.
min(str)	This Python in-built function for String returns the min alphabetical character from the string str.
replace(old, new [, max])	This Python in-built function for String replaces all occurrences of old in string with new or at most max occurrences if max given.
rfind(str, beg=0,end=len(string))	This Python in-built function for String is same as find (), but search backwards in string.
rindex(str, beg=0, end=len(string))	This Python in-built function for String is same as index (), but search backwards in string.

rjust(width,[, fillchar])	This Python in-built function for String returns a space-padded string with the original string right-justified to a total of width columns.
rstrip()	This Python in-built function for String removes all trailing whitespace of string.
split(str="", num=string.count(str))	This Python in-built function for String splits string according to delimiter str (space if not provided) and returns list of substrings; split into at most num substrings if given.
splitlines(num=string.count('\n'))	This Python in-built function for String splits string at all (or num) NEWLINEs and returns a list of each line with NEWLINEs removed.
startswith(str, beg=0,end=len(string))	This Python in-built function for String determines if string or a substring of string (if starting index beg and ending index end are given) starts with substring str; returns true if so and false otherwise.
strip([chars])	This Python in-built function for String performs both lstrip() and rstrip() on string
swapcase()	This Python in-built function for String inverts case for all letters in string.
title()	This Python in-built function for String returns "titlecased" version of string, that is, all words begin with uppercase and the rest are lowercase.

translate(table, deletechars="")	This Python in-built function for String translates string according to translation table str(256 chars), removing those in the del string.
upper()	This Python in-built function for String converts lowercase letters in string to uppercase.
zfill (width)	This Python in-built function for String returns original string leftpadded with zeros to a total of width characters; intended for numbers, zfill () retains any sign given (less one zero).
isdecimal()	This Python in-built function for String returns true if a Unicode string contains only decimal characters and false otherwise.

String Formatting Operator

Python language has the string format operator % which is unique to strings and makes up for the functions present for C language printf (). Following is the list of such operators in Python.

Format Symbol	Conversion
%c	It converts to character
%s	string conversion via str() prior to formatting
%i	It converts to signed decimal integer
%d	It converts to signed decimal integer
%u	It converts to unsigned decimal integer
%o	It converts to octal integer
%x	It converts to hexadecimal integer (lowercase letters)

%X	It converts to hexadecimal integer (upper case letters)
%e	It converts to exponential notation (with lowercase 'e')
%E	It converts to exponential notation (with upper case 'E')
%f	It converts to floating point real number
%g	It converts to the shorter of %f and %e
%G	It converts to the shorter of %f and %E

Python code example for String Formatter

```
StringFormatting ⊠
1  var1 = 'best'
2  var2 = 'language'
3  var3 = 1
4  print ("Python is the %s programming %s. It's No. %d " % (var1, var2, var3))
   <

Console ⊠                                                          ▣ ✖ ✖
<terminated> C:\Python_Workspace\MyFirstPythonProject\src\StringFormatting.py
Python is the best programming language. It's No. 1
```

In the above example %s string formatter is used to format a string and %d is used to format an integer into a string.

Escape Characters

Python language has the following list of escape or non-printable characters that are represented with backslash notation.

An escape character gets interpreted by Python in a single quoted as well as double quoted strings.

Backslash Notation	Hexadecimal Character	Description
\a	0x07	It is used for Bell or alert.
\b	0x08	It is used for Backspace.
\cx		It is used for Control-x.
\C-x		It is used for Control-x.
\e	0x1b	It is used for Escape.
\f	0x0c	It is used for Formfeed.
\M-\C-x		It is used for Meta-Control-x.
\n	0x0a	It is used for Newline.
\nnn		It is used for Octal notation, where n is in the range 0.7.
\r	0x0d	It is used for carriage return.
\s	0x20	It is used for space.
\t	0x09	It is used for tab.
\v	0x0b	It is used for vertical tab.
\x		It is used for character x.
\xnn		It is used for hexadecimal notation, where n is in the range 0.9, a.f, or A.F

Chapter 9
Use of Lists in Python

In chapter 4, we have already discussed about Lists as Python data type. In this chapter we are going to discuss about basic lists operations and Python in-built methods and functions for Lists.

Creating a list

A list in Python can be declared by putting different comma-separated values between square brackets.

e.g. days = ['Sunday', 'Monday', 'Tuesday', 'Wednesday', 'Thursday', 'Friday', 'Saturday']; number = [1, 2, 3, 4, 5,6,7,8,9,0]; chars = ["a", "b", "c", "d", "e"];

Accessing elements from list

Elements from the list can be accessed by using the square brackets for slicing along with the index to procure value available at that index of the list.

E.g. days [1]; number [1:6];

Updating and Adding elements in lists

We can update a single element or multiple elements of a list by giving the slice on the left-hand side of the assignment operator.

E.g. days [2] = 'January';

We can add elements in the list by using the append () method

Deleting an element from list

In Python, we can remove a list element by using the del statement if index is known of the element to be deleted.

E.g. del days [3];

Alternatively, we can use the remove () method to remove an element from a list.

All of these list operations are demonstrated in the below example. First, we created the list. Next, we accessed the elements from the list. Then, we updated 3rd element in the list using the assignment operator. Lastly, we used the del statement to delete an element in the list, doing so days [2] has printed Wednesday as element which was present at days [2] index was deleted.

```
ListOperations ⊠
 1 # Creating lists of elements.
 2 days = ['Sunday', 'Monday', 'Tuesday', 'Wednesday', 'Thursday', 'Friday', 'Saturday']
 3 number = [1, 2, 3, 4, 5,6,7,8,9,0 ]
 4 chars = ["a", "b", "c", "d", "e"]
 5 # Accessing elements from lists.
 6 print("days [1] ", days [1]," number [1:6] ", number [1:6])
 7 # Updating an element in list.
 8 print("days [2] ", days [2])
 9 days [2] = 'January';
10 print("days [2] ", days [2])
11 # Deleting an element from list.
12 del days [2]
13 print("days [2] ", days [2])
```

```
Console ⊠
<terminated> C:\Python_Workspace\MyFirstPythonProject\src\ListOperations.py
days [1]  Monday  number [1:6]  [2, 3, 4, 5, 6]
days [2]  Tuesday
days [2]  January
days [2]  Wednesday
```

Basic lists operations

Like Python strings, we can use + and * operators on lists for operations like concatenation and repetition respectively. Below are the list operations on Python lists.

Python Expression	Results	Description
len([1, 2, 3, 4, 5])	5	Length operation.
[1, 2, 3, 4, 5] + [6, 7, 8, 9, 0]	[1, 2, 3, 4, 5, 6, 7, 8, 9, 0]	Concatenation operation.
['Hello'] * 3	['Hello', 'Hello', 'Hello']	Repetition operation.
4 in [1, 2, 3, 4, 5]	TRUE	Membership operation.

for a in [1, 2, 3, 4, 5]: print a,	1 2 3 4 5	Iteration operation.

Indexing, Slicing, and Matrixes in Lists

Python lists are nothing both sequences, therefore indexing and slicing work the same way for lists as they do for strings. Therefore, below operations are possible.

```
ListSlicing
1  days = ['Sunday', 'Monday', 'Tuesday']
2  print('Offsets start at zero, printing 3rd element ', days[2])
3  print('Negative: count from the right ', days[-2])
4  print('Slicing fetches sections ', days[1:])

Console
<terminated> C:\Python_Workspace\MyFirstPythonProject\src\ListSlicing.py
Offsets start at zero, printing 3rd element  Tuesday
Negative: count from the right  Monday
Slicing fetches sections  ['Monday', 'Tuesday']
```

In the above example, if index is negative then counting will start from the right side and if it starts with 0 then counting will be from left side. Like Python String, Python lists supports slicing and will print the sections of the lists as per their indexes.

Built-in Lists Methods & Functions

Below are Python built-in functions for List operations.

Function	Description
cmp(list1, list2)	This Python built-in function for lists compares elements of both lists.

len(list)	This Python built-in function for lists gives the total length of the list.
max(list)	This Python built-in function for lists returns item from the list with max value.
min(list)	This Python built-in function for lists returns item from the list with min value.
list(seq)	This Python built-in function for lists converts a tuple into list.

Chapter 10
Use of Tuples

In the chapter 4, we have already mentioned Tuples as Python data type and some details about it. In this chapter, we are going to discuss about basic tuples operations and Python in-built methods and functions for Tuples.

Creating a Tuple

A tuple is a sequence of immutable Python objects. A tuple in Python can be declared by putting different comma-separated values between parentheses.

e.g. days = ('Sunday', 'Monday', 'Tuesday', 'Wednesday', 'Thursday', 'Friday', 'Saturday'); number = (1, 2, 3, 4, 5,6,7,8,9,0); chars = ("a", "b", "c", "d", "e");

Accessing elements from Tuples

Elements from the tuple can be accessed by using the square brackets for slicing along with the index to procure value available at that index of the tuple.

E.g. days [1]; number [1:6];

Updating and Adding elements in Tuples

We cannot modify any element of a tuple as tuples are immutable which means we cannot update or change the values or size of tuple elements.

Deleting an element from Tuples

It is not possible to remove an individual tuple element from a tuple as tuples are immutable. However, we can remove an entire tuple by just using the 'del' statement.

All of these tuples operations are demonstrated in the below example. First, we created the tuples. Next, we accessed the elements from the tuples. We cannot update the value of any element in Tuple. Lastly, we used the 'del' statement to delete the entire tuple, when attempted to print the deleted tuple it throws an error as it no longer exists in memory.

```
TupleOperations
 1  # Creation of tuples
 2  days = ('Sunday', 'Monday', 'Tuesday', 'Wednesday', 'Thursday', 'Friday', 'Saturday')
 3  number = (1, 2, 3, 4, 5,6,7,8,9,0 )
 4  chars = ("a", "b", "c", "d", "e")
 5  # Accessing value from tuple
 6  print("days [1] ", days [1]," number [1:6] ", number [1:6])
 7  # Updating an element in tuple
 8  # Not allowed as Tuples are immutable
 9  # Deleting entire tuple
10  del chars
11  print(chars)
```

```
Console
<terminated> C:\Python_Workspace\MyFirstPythonProject\src\TupleOperations.py
days [1]  Monday  number [1:6]  (2, 3, 4, 5, 6)
Traceback (most recent call last):
  File "C:\Python_Workspace\MyFirstPythonProject\src\TupleOperations.py", line 11, in <module>
    print(chars)
NameError: name 'chars' is not defined
```

Basic Tuples operations

Like Python strings, we can use + and * operators on tuples for operations like concatenation and repetition respectively. Below are the tuples operations on Python tuples.

Python Expression	Results	Description
len((1, 2, 3, 4, 5))	5	Length operation.
(1, 2, 3, 4, 5)+ (6, 7, 8, 9, 0)	(1, 2, 3, 4, 5, 6, 7, 8, 9, 0)	Concatenation operation.
('Hello') * 3	('Hello', 'Hello', 'Hello')	Repetition operation.
4 in (1, 2, 3, 4, 5)	TRUE	Membership operation.
for a in (1, 2, 3, 4, 5): print a,	1 2 3 4 5	Iteration operation.

Indexing, Slicing, and Matrixes in Tuples

Python tuples are nothing but sequences, therefore indexing and slicing work the same way for tuples as they do for strings. Therefore, below operations are possible.

```
TupleSlicing ✕
1  days = ('Sunday', 'Monday', 'Tuesday')
2  print('Offsets start at zero, printing 3rd element ', days[2])
3  print('Negative: count from the right ', days[-2])
4  print('Slicing fetches sections ', days[1:])
```

```
Console ✕
<terminated> C:\Python_Workspace\MyFirstPythonProject\src\TupleSlicing.py
Offsets start at zero, printing 3rd element  Tuesday
Negative: count from the right  Monday
Slicing fetches sections  ('Monday', 'Tuesday')
```

In the above example, if index is negative then counting will start from right side. If it starts with 0 then counting will be from left side. Like Python String, Python tuples supports slicing and will print the sections of the tuples as per their indexes.

Built-in Tuples Methods & Functions

Below are Python built-in functions for Tuples operations.

Function	Description
cmp(tuple1, tuple2)	This Python built-in function for tuples compares elements of both tuples.
len(tuple)	This Python built-in function for tuples gives the total length of the tuple.
max(tuple)	This Python built-in function for tuples returns item from the tuple with max value.
min(tuple)	This Python built-in function for tuples returns item from the tuple with min value.
tuple(seq)	This Python built-in function for tuples converts a list into tuple.

Chapter 11

Use of Dictionary

In the chapter 4, we saw basics of Dictionary as Python data type. In this chapter, we are going to discuss about dictionary operations and Python in-built methods and functions for dictionary.

Creating a Dictionary

A Python dictionary can be created by placing key value pairs separated by comma within the curly braces as shown in the below example.

E.g. biodata = {'Name': 'Julie', 'Age': 25, 'Height': '180cm', 'Profession': 'Banker'};

Accessing elements from Dictionary

Element values from dictionary can be procured by using square brackets along with the key in it as shown in the below example.

E.g. biodata ['Profession']; biodata ['Age'];

Updating and Adding elements in Dictionary

In Python language, a new entry of key value pair can be done by adding a new key value pair with the name of the dictionary as shown in the below example.

E.g. biodata ['Company'] = "XYZ Ltd.";

An existing value in dictionary can be updated by using the assignment operator and assign a new value to the key element in the dictionary as shown in the below example.

E.g. biodata ['Age'] = 22;

Deleting an element from Dictionary

In Python language, a complete key-value pair element can be deleted by using 'del' statement before square brackets along with the key in it which is to be deleted as shown in the below example.

E.g. del biodata ['Company'];

Also, if we want to delete the entire dictionary, it can be done by using the 'del' statement before dictionary variable as shown in the below example.

E.g. del biodata;

In the below Python code example, firstly, we have created dictionaries (biodata and month). Secondly, we are accessing element values from dictionary. Thirdly, we are adding key value pair in dictionary and then updating the value of one of the key-value pair in dictionary. Lastly, we have deleted an entire key value pair from dictionary based on its key and the complete dictionary using 'del' statement.

```
DictionaryOperation ⊠
1  # Creating dictionary
2  biodata = {'Name' : 'Julie','Age' : 25,'Height' : '180cm','Profession' : 'Banker'}
3  month = {'First':'January','Second':'February','Third':'March'}
4  # Accessing values into dictionary
5  print("Accessing element from dictionary biodata ['Profession'] ",biodata ['Profession']);
6  print("Accessing element from dictionary biodata ['Age'] ",biodata ['Age'])
7  #Updating Values in Dictionary
8  biodata['Age']=22
9  print("Update Age in dictionary is ",biodata['Age'])
10 # Adding key value pair in dictionary
11 biodata['Company']='XYZ Ltd.'
12 print("New added element in dictionary biodata['Company'] ",biodata['Company'])
13 # deleting Values from dictionary
14 print("Dictionary before deleting elements.");print(biodata)
15 del biodata['Company']
16 print("Dictionary After deleting elements.");print(biodata)
17 # deleting the dictionary
18 del month; print(month)
```

```
Console ⊠                                                    ▣ ✕ ✕ ℚ 🐚 ▏🔖 🔖
<terminated> C:\Python_Workspace\MyFirstPythonProject\src\DictionaryOperation.py
Accessing element from dictionary biodata ['Profession']  Banker
Accessing element from dictionary biodata ['Age']  25
Update Age in dictionary is  22
New added element in dictionary biodata['Company']  XYZ Ltd.
Dictionary before deleting elements.
{'Profession': 'Banker', 'Company': 'XYZ Ltd.', 'Name': 'Julie', 'Age': 22, 'Height': '180cm'}
Dictionary After deleting elements.
{'Profession': 'Banker', 'Name': 'Julie', 'Age': 22, 'Height': '180cm'}
Traceback (most recent call last):
  File "C:\Python_Workspace\MyFirstPythonProject\src\DictionaryOperation.py", line 18, in <module>
    del month; print(month)
NameError: name 'month' is not defined
```

Properties of Dictionary Keys

> ➢ Key cannot be duplicated. Therefore only one entry per key is permitted in Python dictionary. If python interpreter encounters duplicate keys during assignment, the last assignment wins i.e. will be considered or overwrite the previous one.

> ➢ Keys in dictionary are immutable. It means we can use numbers, strings or tuples as dictionary keys but anything like ['key'] is not allowed in Python dictionary data type.

Built-in Dictionary Functions & Methods

Below are Python built-in function for dictionary.

Function	Description
cmp(dict1, dict2)	This Python built-in function for dictionary compares elements of both dict.
len(dict)	This Python built-in function for dictionary gives the total length of the dictionary. This would be equal to the number of items in the dictionary.
str(dict)	This Python built-in function for dictionary produces a printable string representation of a dictionary
type(variable)	This Python built-in function for dictionary returns the type of the passed variable. If passed variable is dictionary, then it would return a dictionary type.

Below are Python built-in methods for dictionary.

Methods	Description
dict.clear()	This Python built-in method for dictionary removes all elements of dictionary dict
dict.copy()	This Python built-in method for dictionary returns a shallow copy of dictionary dict
dict.fromkeys()	This Python built-in method for dictionary create a new dictionary with keys from seq and values set to value.

dict.get(key, default=None)	For key 'key', returns value or default if key not in dictionary
dict.has_key(key)	This Python built-in method for dictionary returns true if key in dictionary dict, false otherwise
dict.items()	This Python built-in method for dictionary returns a list of dict's (key, value) tuple pairs
dict.keys()	This Python built-in method for dictionary returns list of dictionary dict's keys
dict.setdefault(key, default=None)	This Python built-in method for dictionary is similar to get(), but will set dict[key]=default if key is not already in dict
dict.update(dict2)	This Python built-in method for dictionary adds dictionary dict2's key-values pairs to dict
dict.values()	This Python built-in method for dictionary returns list of dictionary dict's values

Chapter 12

Date and Time

In Python programming language, date and time can be handled in the following ways.

Tick

Tick in Python is the instance if time measured in seconds since January 1, 1970 12:00. Python has time module which has functions to work with time. The function time.time () returns the current system time in ticks since 12:00am, January 1, 1970(epoch) as shown in the below example.

```
Tick
1  import time;  # time module is required for this operation.
2
3  ticks = time.time()
4  print ("Number of ticks happened since January 1, 1970 12:00 are ", ticks)
5
```

```
Console
<terminated> C:\Python_Workspace\MyFirstPythonProject\src\Tick.py
Number of ticks happened since January 1, 1970 12:00 are  1461723587.147774
```

TimeTuple

In Python language, many time functions handle time as a tuple of 9 numbers as indicated in the below table. This tuple is equivalent to struct_time structure shown in the attribute column.

Index	Field	Values	Attributes
0	4-digit year	2008	tm_year
1	Month	1 to 12	tm_mon
2	Day	1 to 31	tm_mday
3	Hour	0 to 23	tm_hour
4	Minute	0 to 59	tm_min
5	Second	0 to 61 (60 or 61 are leap-seconds)	tm_sec
6	Day of Week	0 to 6 (0 is Monday)	tm_wday
7	Day of year	1 to 366 (Julian day)	tm_yday
8	Daylight savings	(-1, 0, 1, -1) means library determines DST	tm_isdst

Python code example for TimeTuple

- **Getting current local time:** To get the current local time in TimeTuple format use the function as time.localtime(time.time()), this function will translate the tick seconds into struct_time structure as a tuple of 9 numbers as discussed above.

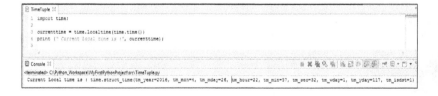

- **Formatting current local time:** To get the current local readable format use the function as time.asctime () as shown in the below example.

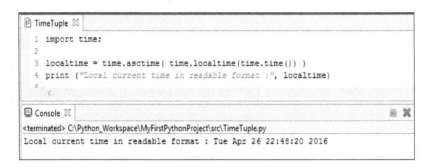

- **Print calendar for a month:** Python has a calendar module which gives a wide range of methods to work with monthly and yearly calendars. In the below example, we are going to print a calendar for a Feb 2016 month (leap year) using the function calendar.month (year, month).

```
P Calendar ⊠
  1  import calendar
  2
  3  calen = calendar.month(2016, 2)
  4  print ("Below is the calendar for Feb 2016.")
  5  print (calen)
     <
```

```
Console ⊠                                                                    ▪ X
<terminated> C:\Python_Workspace\MyFirstPythonProject\src\Calendar.py
Below is the calendar for Feb 2016.
    February 2016
Mo Tu We Th Fr Sa Su
 1  2  3  4  5  6  7
 8  9 10 11 12 13 14
15 16 17 18 19 20 21
22 23 24 25 26 27 28
29
```

Summary of functions in Time Module

Below are the functions available in Calendar module.

Time Functions	Description
time.altzone	This is to be used only when Only use this if daylight is nonzero. It is positive if the offset of the local DST time zone is west of UTC. This is negative if the local DST time zone is east of UTC (as in Western Europe, including the UK). All in seconds.
time.asctime([tupletime])	This function of time module accepts a time-tuple and returns a readable 24-character string such as 'Tue Apr 26 19:09:19 2016'.

time.clock( )	This function of time module returns the current CPU time as a floating-point number of seconds.
time.ctime([seconds])	This function of time module is just like function asctime (localtime (seconds)) and without arguments is like asctime( ).
time.gmtime([seconds])	This function of time module accepts an instant expressed in seconds since the epoch and returns a time-tuple xyz with the UTC time. It is to be noted that zyz.tm_isdst is always 0.
time.localtime([seconds])	This function of time module accepts an instant expressed in seconds since the epoch and returns a time-tuple t with the local time (t.tm_isdst is 0 or 1, depending on whether DST applies to instant secs by local rules).
time.mktime(tupletime)	This function of time module accepts an instant expressed as a time-tuple in local time. It returns a floating-point value with the instant expressed in seconds since the epoch.
time.sleep(secs)	This function of time module suspends the calling thread for secs seconds.
time.strftime(fmt[,tuplet ime])	This function of time module accepts an instant expressed as a time-tuple in local time. It returns a string representing the instant as specified by string fmt.

time.strptime(strg,format='%a %b %d %H:%M:%S %Y')	This function of time module parses strg according to format string format. It returns the instant in time-tuple format.
time.time( )	As discussed in above examples, this function of time module returns the current time instant, a floating-point number of seconds since the epoch.
time.tzset()	This function of time module resets the time conversion rules used by the library routines.

Summary of functions in Calendar Module

Below are the functions available in Calendar module.

Calendar Functions	Description
calendar.calendar(year, width=2,line=1,space=6)	This function of calendar module returns a multiline string with a calendar for *year* year formatted into three columns separated by *space* spaces, *width* is the width in characters of each date; each line has length 21*width+18+2*c. *line* is the number of lines for each week.
calendar.firstweekday( )	This function of calendar module returns the current setting for the weekday that starts each week. Default value is 0, which is Monday.
calendar.isleap(year)	This function of calendar module returns True if it is a leap year; otherwise, False.

calendar.leapdays(ye1,ye 2)	This function of calendar module returns the total number of leap days in the years within range (ye1, ye2).
calendar.month(year, month, width=2,line=1)	This function of calendar module returns a multiline string with a calendar for month month of year year, one line per week plus two header lines. width is the width in characters of each date; each line has length 7*w+6. line is the number of lines for each week.
calendar.monthcalendar(year, month)	This function of calendar module returns a list of lists of ints. Each such sublist denotes a week. Days outside 'month' month of 'year' year are set to 0; days within the month are set to their day-of-month, 1 and up.
calendar.monthrange(yea r, month)	This function of calendar module returns two integers. The first one is the code of the weekday for the first day of the month month in year year; the second one is the number of days in the month. Month numbers are 1 (January) to 12 (December). Weekday codes are 0 (Monday) to 6 (Sunday).
calendar.prcal(year,w=2,l =1,c=6)	This function of calendar module works like print calendar.calendar (year,w,l,c).
calendar.prmonth(year,m onth,w=2,l=1)	This function of calendar module works like print calendar.month (year,month,w,l).

calendar.setfirstweekday(weekday)	This function of calendar module sets the first day of each week to weekday code weekday. Month numbers are 1 (January) to 12 (December). Weekday codes are 0 (Monday) to 6 (Sunday).
calendar.timegm(tupleti me)	The inverse of time.gmtime: accepts a time instant in time-tuple form and returns the same instant as a floating-point number of seconds since the epoch.
calendar.weekday(year, month, day)	This function of calendar module returns the weekday code for the given date. Month numbers are 1 (January) to 12 (December). Weekday codes are 0 (Monday) to 6 (Sunday).

Chapter 13

Use of functions

As we have seen in previous chapters, Python has many in-built functions and the popular print () function is one of those functions. Similarly, we can create our own functions known as user defined functions (UDF). A function may be defined as a block of code that is well organized and reusable multiple times to perform a number of operations in a program that demands high modularity and reusability.

Syntax of a Python function

> *def functionname (parameters or arguments):*
>
> *"docstring"*
>
> *Block of code or indented statements*
>
> *return [expression]*

Rules to define a Python function

➤ A function block has a structure which starts with keyword def followed by the name of function and parentheses ().

➤ Parentheses can have number of input arguments or parameters within it. Also, we can define values for these parameters inside these parentheses.

> Python function can have its first statement as an optional statement known as the *docstring* or the documentation string of that function.

> A code block within a Python function starts with a colon (:) and all statements in the block are indented.

> A Python function ends with return [expression], this exits a function returning an expression value and control to the caller. A return may or may not return an expression value.

Calling a Python function

Python function can be called anywhere in the program with function name and passing the values to its parameters. This is to be made sure that we should send equal number of values to equal number of parameters i.e. if there is one parameter in a function then we just need to send one value, similarly if there are two parameters then we need to send two values and so on. Such type of parameters are also known as required arguments to a function. Below is an example that demonstrates calling of a Python function.

```
 PythonFunctionDemo

1  def printString (strg):
2      "This is user defined Python function to print a String."
3      print(strg)
4      return
5
6  #We can call this function with its name as follows.
7  printString("Calling first time!")
8  printString("Calling second time!")
9  printString("Calling third time!")

 Console
<terminated> C:\Python_Workspace\MyFirstPythonProject\src\PythonFunctionDemo.py
Calling first time!
Calling second time!
Calling third time!
```

Passing by reference vs Passing by value

All parameters or arguments in Python are passed by reference. Therefore, if we change a parameter that refers to within a function, this change will be reflected in the actual calling function as shown in the below example.

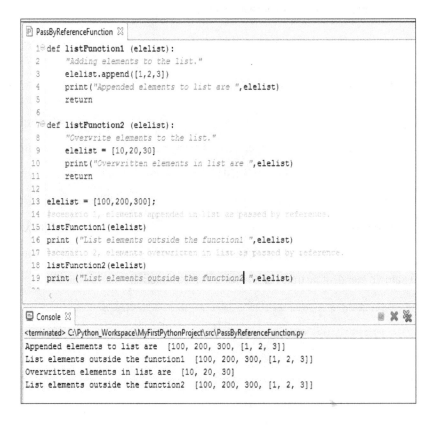

```
P PassByReferenceFunction ⌘

1  def listFunction1 (elelist):
2      "Adding elements to the list."
3      elelist.append([1,2,3])
4      print("Appended elements to list are ",elelist)
5      return
6
7  def listFunction2 (elelist):
8      "Overwrite elements to the list."
9      elelist = [10,20,30]
10     print("Overwritten elements in list are ",elelist)
11     return
12
13 elelist = [100,200,300];
14 #scenario 1, elements appended in list as passed by reference.
15 listFunction1(elelist)
16 print ("List elements outside the function1 ",elelist)
17 #scenario 2, elements overwritten in list as passed by reference.
18 listFunction2(elelist)
19 print ("List elements outside the function2 ",elelist)
```

```
Console ⌘                                                          ▦ ✖ ✖

<terminated> C:\Python_Workspace\MyFirstPythonProject\src\PassByReferenceFunction.py
Appended elements to list are  [100, 200, 300, [1, 2, 3]]
List elements outside the function1  [100, 200, 300, [1, 2, 3]]
Overwritten elements in list are  [10, 20, 30]
List elements outside the function2  [100, 200, 300, [1, 2, 3]]
```

In the second case, although we have passed arguments by reference the change of list overwritten is visible only in the local scope (parameter elelist) of the function yet outside the function the actual list remains unaffected as shown in the above example for listFunction2.

Python function arguments

A function in Python can be called with the following types of formal arguments.

> **Required arguments:** In case of the required arguments, the arguments to a function are passed in correct positional order. Therefore, the number of arguments defined in a function should match exactly the number of arguments passed to that function. If there is mismatch, system will throw an error as shown in the below example.

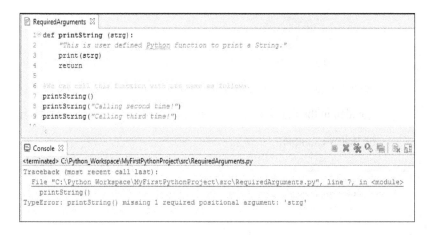

> **Keyword arguments:** In python, when we use keyword argument in a function call then the caller identifies the arguments by its name. This feature of Python, provides the flexibility to place the arguments out of order as Python interpreter uses the keywords to match the values with parameters. This is demonstrated in the below example. Here we have

entered arguments which are out of sequence with parameter but interpreter by using the keywords processed them correctly.

```
KeywordArgument ⬚
  1  def printStrings (strg, numb):
  2      "This is user defined Python function to print a String."
  3      print("First Argument is ",strg)
  4      print("Second Argument is ",numb)
  5      return
  6
  7  #We can call this function with its name as follows.
  8  printStrings(numb = 3, strg = "First String")
  9
```
```
Console ⬚
<terminated> C:\Python_Workspace\MyFirstPythonProject\src\KeywordArgument.py
First Argument is  First String
Second Argument is  3
```

> **Default arguments:** Python has a feature of the default arguments. Default argument assumes a default value if a value is defaulted or not provided in the function call for that argument. This is demonstrated in the below example.

```
DefaultArgument ⬚
  1  def printStrings (name, age, gender = 'Female'):
  2      "This is user defined Python function to print a String."
  3      print("Name is ",name)
  4      print("Gender is ",gender)
  5      print("Age is ",age)
  6      return
  7
  8  #We can call this function with its name as follows.
  9  printStrings(age = 32, name = "Martin", gender = 'Male')
 10  printStrings(age = 32, name = "Julie")
 11
```
```
Console ⬚
<terminated> C:\Python_Workspace\MyFirstPythonProject\src\DefaultArgument.py
Name is  Martin
Gender is  Male
Age is  32
Name is  Julie
Gender is  Female
Age is  32
```

➤ **Variable-length arguments:** Python supports the feature of specifying variable length arguments. These arguments are not named in the function definition as compared to required and default arguments. The syntax and example for variable-length arguments are shown below.

```
def functionname([formal_args,] *var_args_tuple ):

"docstring"

Block of code or statements

return [expression]
```

In the below example, during the first function call when single argument is passed, it just printed that argument and variable-length argument remained untouched. In the next example, when three arguments are passed then variable-length argument parsed the additional arguments and helped program to print them.

```
P VariableLengthArgument ⊠
 1  # Function definition is here
 2⊖ def printInformation( arg1, *variabletuple ):
 3      "This function prints the information passed in variable length argument"
 4      print ("Output is: ")
 5      print (arg1)
 6      for variables in variabletuple:
 7          print (variables)
 8      return;
 9
10  # Calling printInformation function
11  printInformation( 100 )
12  printInformation( 200, 300, 400)
    <
```

```
Console ⊠                                                                    ⊞ ✖ ✖
<terminated> C:\Python_Workspace\MyFirstPythonProject\src\VariableLengthArgument.py
Output is:
100
Output is:
200
300
400
```

Python Anonymous Functions

When function in Python are not declared in the standard manner using *def* keyword but with use of *lambda* keyword are known as Anonymous functions in Python. Syntax is shown below:

Syntax

> *lambda [arg1 [,arg2,......argn]]:expression*

Below are the features of the anonymous function.

> ➤ Lambda can accept any number of arguments but return just one value as expression. They do not contain multiple expressions or commands.

> Since lambda requires an expression therefore, anonymous function cannot make a direct call to print.

> Lambda functions can have their own local namespace but cannot access variables other than those present in their parameter list and in the global namespace.

Below is an example of anonymous function.

```
  VariableLengthArgument       AnonymousFunction 

  1  # Anonymous Function definition is here.
  2  subtract = lambda arg1, arg2: arg1 - arg2;
  3
  4  # call subtract as a function
  5  print ("Value of total : ", subtract( 90, 30 ))
  6  print ("Value of total : ", subtract( 50, 25 ))

  Console 

<terminated> C:\Python_Workspace\MyFirstPythonProject\src\AnonymousFunction.py
Value of total :    60
Value of total :    25
```

Python *return* Statement

Using return statement in Python, we can return a value as expression and the control back to the caller. Below is an example.

```
ⓟ ReturnStatement ⊠
 1  # Function definition
 2⊕ def addition (arg1, arg2):
 3      "This function does the addition of two numbers"
 4      arg3 = arg1 + arg2
 5      return arg3
 6⊕ def subtraction (arg1, arg2):
 7      "This function does the addition of two numbers"
 8      arg3 = arg1 - arg2
 9      return arg3
10⊕ def multiplication (arg1, arg2):
11      "This function does the addition of two numbers"
12      arg3 = arg1 * arg2
13      return arg3
14
15  # Call all functions from here
16  print ("Result of addition is ", addition(200,100))
17  print ("Result of subtraction is ", subtraction(200,100))
18  print ("Result of multiplication is ", multiplication(200,100))
    <
```

```
🖳 Console ⊠                                                          ▣ ✖ ✖
<terminated> C:\Python_Workspace\MyFirstPythonProject\src\ReturnStatement.py
Result of addition is   300
Result of subtraction is   100
Result of multiplication is   20000
```

Scope of Variables in Python

There are two scopes of variables defined in Python.

> **Global Variables:** These are the variables defined outside the function body and can be accessed from anywhere within the program.

> **Local Variables:** These are the variables defined inside the function body and have a local scope of accessibility.

Below is the example to demonstrate local and global scope of a variable in Python.

```
  VariableScope ⊠
  1  total = 89   # This is a global scope variable
  2  # Function Definition
  3  def addition (arg1, arg2):
  4      "This function does the addition of two numbers"
  5      total = arg1 + arg2   # total here is a local scope variable
  6      return total
  7
  8  # Call all functions from here
  9  print ("Result of addition is ", addition(200,100))
 10  print (total)
```

```
  Console ⊠                                                    ▣ ✖ ✖
<terminated> C:\Python_Workspace\MyFirstPythonProject\src\VariableScope.py
Result of addition is   300
89
```

In the above example, the variable total present inside the function has a local scope and the variable total declared at the top of the program has global scope. When both of the variable values printed shows the different result due to their accessibility scope.

Chapter 14

Use of Modules

In this chapter, we are going to learn about modules in Python language. Modules allows us to logically organize our Python code which makes the code easier to understand and use. In Python language, a module is just a file consisting of Python code which has several in-built or user defined functions.

Python *import* Statement

We can call the Python code or functions present in a file as module by using the import statement followed by the Python file name. Below is the syntax for import statement in Python.

```
import module1[, module2[,... moduleN]
```

Below is an example to work in Python modules.

Creating a Python file to be used as module.

```
ReturnStatement ☒
1    # Function definition
2    def addition (arg1, arg2):
3        "This function does the addition of two numbers"
4        arg3 = arg1 + arg2
5        return arg3
6    def subtraction (arg1, arg2):
7        "This function does the addition of two numbers"
8        arg3 = arg1 - arg2
9        return arg3
10   def multiplication (arg1, arg2):
11       "This function does the addition of two numbers"
12       arg3 = arg1 * arg2
13       return arg3
14
```

Calling the above module and operating on the user defined function in the current Python program is shown in the below example.

```
ReturnStatement   PythonModules ☒
1    # Using import statement to include functions from existing Python file
2    import ReturnStatement
3
4    # Call all functions from here
5    print ("Result of addition is ", ReturnStatement.addition(200,100))
6    print ("Result of subtraction is ", ReturnStatement.subtraction(200,100))
7    print ("Result of multiplication is ", ReturnStatement.multiplication(200,100))
8

Console ☒
<terminated> C:\Python_Workspace\MyFirstPythonProject\src\PythonModules.py
Result of addition is  300
Result of subtraction is  100
Result of multiplication is  20000
```

Python from...import Statement

In Python language, from...import statement lets us import only specific and not all attributes from a module into the current namespace. It has the following syntax −

```
from modulename import name1[, name2[, ... nameN]]
```

For example, if we need to import only the function addition from the above module *ReturnStatement*, then we use the following statement – *from ReturnStatement import addition*

This statement does not import the entire module *ReturnStatement* into the current namespace but it just introduces the function *addition* from the module *ReturnStatement* into the global symbol table of the importing module. This is demonstrated in the below example.

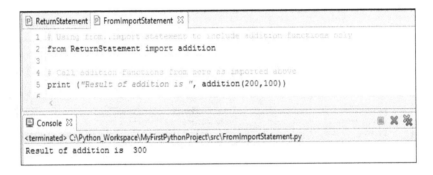

Python from…import* Statement

Using this Python statement, we can import all names or functions from a module into the current namespace. It has the following syntax.

*from modulename import ***

Although, it provides an easy way to import everything from a module into the current namespace yet this statement is used rarely.

Locating Python Modules

In Python, when we import a module, the Python interpreter searches for the module in the following sequences. First in the current directory, if that module isn't located then Python searches each directory in the shell variable PYTHONPATH. If it fails here as well then lastly Python checks the default path.

Search path for module is stored in the system module sys as the sys.path variable. The sys.path variable contains the current directory, PYTHONPATH, and the installation-dependent default.

The PYTHONPATH Variable:

The PYTHONPATH is an environment variable that consists of a list of directories. Below are the syntaxes of PYTHONPATH for Windows and UNIX.

PYTHONPATH from a Windows system:

set PYTHONPATH=c:\Python34\lib;

PYTHONPATH from a UNIX system:

set PYTHONPATH=/usr/local/lib/python

Python in-built functions for Modules

Below are the in-built Python functions that are used while working with modules.

Functions	Description
dir( )	The dir () Python built-in function returns a sorted list of strings containing the names defined by a module. E.g. if module name is math then dir (math) will list down all the names present in that module.
globals()	If Python in-built function globals () is called from within a function then it will return all the names (as dictionary datatype) that can be accessed globally from that function.
locals()	If Python in-built function locals () is called from within a function then it will return all the names (as dictionary datatype) that can be accessed locally from that function.
reload()	In Python, when we import a module into a script, the code in the top-level portion of a module is executed only once. Therefore, if we want to execute the top-level code in a module again, then we have to use the reload () function. This function imports a previously imported module again.

Packages in Python

In Python, a package may be defined as a hierarchical file directory structure which defines a single Python application environment that consists of modules, sub-packages and so on.

Using eclipse, we can give the package name when we are creating a new Python program file as shown in the below screenshot.

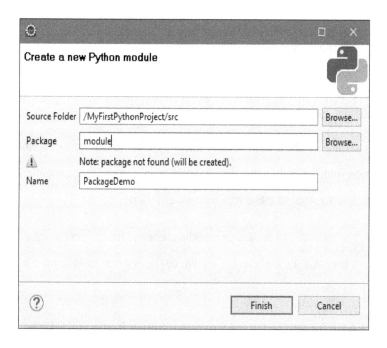

After click of finish button, a new package with name as module will be created along with _init_.py file as shown in the below screenshot.

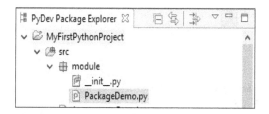

In order to make all of our existing required functions available for files present within a new package, we import Python file present at PYTHONPATH in this in __init__.py file. For this we need to put explicit import statements in __init__.py as shown in the below example.

```
  PackageDemo   module ⊠   ReturnStatement
 1   from ReturnStatement import addition
 2
 3
 4
     <
```

After setting up above import in __init__.py file, we can now call *addition* function from the Python program that present in a new package *module*. Only things that we need to make sure here are as follows.

> First we need to declare import statement and the current package name where this file is present. This will be the first statement in the program file.

> Next, we can call the existing function (already imported) starting with current package name (e.g., module.addition (4, 5)).

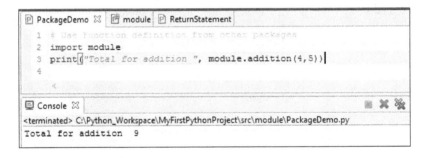

Chapter 15

File I/O used in Python

In the previous chapters, we have already learnt to use print function for printing the output on screen or console. In this we chapter we are going to learn about I/O (accepting input and printing output on console) and basic file operations.

Python print Function

By using simple print function as *print (set of strings or variables),* the system will print the content on to the console.

E.g., print ("Hello World!")

Python input Function

Python has *input ([prompt])* as its in-built function that read one line from standard input assuming it as a valid Python expression and returns it to the system as a string. Below is an example.

```
  RawInput ⊠
  1  strg = input("Please enter your input: ");
  2  print ("We have received input as : ", strg)
  3
```

```
  Console ⊠
  <terminated> C:\Python_Workspace\MyFirstPythonProject\src\RawInput.py
  Please enter your input: Hello Python
  We have received input as :  Hello Python
```

Opening and Closing files in Python

Python language provides basic functions and methods which are necessary to manipulate files by default. We can do the file manipulation in Python by using a file object.

The open () Function

Python has in-built open () function that creates a file object with which we can read or write a file and call other support methods associated with it.

Syntax

> *file object = open(file_name [, access_mode][, Buffering])*

Description of the parameter in detail:

> **file_name:** It is a string value that contains the name of the file that we want to access.

> **access_mode:** It determines the mode in which the file has to be opened, i.e., write, read, append, etc. Given below is the complete list of possible values in the table. This parameter is optional with default file access mode as read (r).

Modes	Description
r	This mode opens a file in read only mode. Beginning of the file has the file pointer. This is the default mode.

rb	This mode opens a file in read only mode in binary format. Beginning of the file has the file pointer. This is the default mode.
r+	This mode opens a file in both reading and writing mode. Beginning of the file has the file pointer.
rb+	This mode opens a file in both reading and writing mode in binary format. Beginning of the file has the file pointer.
w	This mode opens a file in writing only mode. It overwrites the file if the file exists. If the file does not exist then it creates a new file for writing.
wb	This ode opens a file in writing only mode in binary format. It overwrites the file if the file exists. If the file does not exist then it creates a new file for writing.
w+	This mode opens a file in both writing and reading mode. It overwrites the existing file if the file exists. If the file does not exist then it creates a new file for reading and writing.
wb+	This mode opens a file in both writing and reading mode in binary format. It overwrites the existing file if the file exists. If the file does not exist then it creates a new file for reading and writing.
a	This mode opens a file for appending. The file pointer is present at the end of the file if the file exists. If the file does not exist then it creates a new file for writing.
ab	This mode opens a file for appending in binary format. The file pointer is at the end of the file if the file exists. If the file does not exist then it it creates a new file for writing.
a+	This mode opens a file for both appending and reading. The file pointer is at the end of the file if the file exists. If the file does not exist then it it creates a new file for reading and writing.
ab+	This mode opens a file for both appending and reading in binary format. The file pointer is at the end of the file if the file exists. If the file does not exist then it creates a new file for reading and writing.

> **Buffering:** It can have value as negative, 0, 1, 2, etc. Depending on these values, if it is set to 0 then no buffering takes place. If it is set to 1 then line buffering is performed while accessing a file. If this

buffering value as an integer greater than 1 then buffering action takes place with the indicated buffer size. If the value is negative then the buffer size has the system default behavior.

The file Object Attributes

When a data file is opened then we get a file object using which we get various information related to that file.

Given below are the file attributes which provide the information associated with the file object.

Attribute	Description
file.closed	This attribute returns true if file is closed, otherwise false.
file.mode	This attribute returns access mode with which file was opened.
file.name	This attribute returns name of the file.
file.softspace	This attribute returns false if space explicitly required with print, otherwise true.

Below is the example for reading file Attributes from a file object.

```
filedemo.txt 🗙    FileAttribute 🗙
  1  # Open a file
  2  file = open("filedemo.txt", "wb")
  3  print ("Name of the file: ", file.name)
  4  print ("File is Closed or not : ", file.closed)
  5  print ("Opening mode of file : ", file.mode)
  6
  <

Console 🗙                                                          ⬛ ✖ ✖✖
<terminated> C:\Python_Workspace\MyFirstPythonProject\src\FileAttribute.py
Name of the file:  filedemo.txt
File is Closed or not :  False
Opening mode of file :  wb
```

Python in-built Methods for File Operations

Below table has the in-built function name and description for a file.

Methods	Description
close()	The close () method of a file object flushes any unwritten information and closes the file object. Once file is closed the no more writing can be done. *E.g. fileObject.close ().*
write()	The write () method writes string data to an open file. Python strings can have binary data as well as text. It is to be note that the write () method does not add a newline character ('\n') to the end of the string. E.g. fileObject.write (string).
read()	The read () method reads a string data from an open file. Python strings can have binary data as well as text data. *E.g. fileObject.read ([count]);* count is the passed parameter which represents the number of bytes to be read from the opened file. If count is missing, then it tries to read data from file as much as possible until the end of file.
tell()	The function tell () method tells us about the current position within the file. It tells us about position of the next read or write of string data at that many bytes from the beginning of the file. *E.g. fileObject.tell ().*

seek(offset[, from])	The function seek (offset [, from]) is used to change the current file position. The offset argument indicates the number of bytes that to be moved. The 'from' argument specifies the reference position from where the bytes are required to be moved. If from has value set to 0, it means use the beginning of the file as the reference position and it has value set to 1 means use the current position as the reference position and if it has value set to 2 then the end of the file would be taken as the reference position. E.g. fileObject.seek (0, 0).
rename()	The rename () method takes two arguments, the current filename and the new filename. E.g. fileObject.rename (current_file_name, new_file_name).
remove()	The remove () method is used to delete files by supplying the name. It can be used to delete files by supplying the name of the file to be deleted as the argument. E.g. fileObject.remove (current_file_name).
mkdir()	The mkdir () method of the os module is used to create directories in the current directory. We need to supply an argument to this method that contains the name of the directory to be created. E.g. os.mkdir ("newdir").
chdir()	The chdir () method is used to change the current directory. The chdir () method takes an argument, that is the name of the directory that you want to make the current directory. E.g. os.chdir ("newdir").
getcwd()	The getcwd () method is used to display the current working directory. E.g. os.getcwd ().
rmdir()	The rmdir () method is used to delete the directory, which is passed as an argument in the method. E.g. os.rmdir ('dirname').

Example on file operations using Python in-built file methods

```
  filedemo.txt        FileOpeartions ⊠
   1  # Open a file in read mode
   2  fileObject = open("filedemo.txt", "r+")
   3  print ("Name of the file: ", fileObject.name)
   4  # Reading the file content
   5  print (fileObject.read(10))
   6  fileObject.close() #closing the current file
   7  # Writing content in a file in append mode
   8  fileObject1 = open("filedemo.txt", "a+")
   9  # Writing Content to a file
  10  fileObject1.write("Hello Python!")
  11  print("Current file pointer position is ", fileObject1.tell())
  12  #Seeking file pointer to the beginning
  13  fileObject1.seek(0,0)
  14  print("Current file pointer position is ", fileObject1.tell())
  15  print (fileObject1.read(100))
  16  fileObject1.close()   # closing the current file
  17
     <
```

```
  Console ⊠                                                          ▣ ✖ ✖
<terminated> C:\Python_Workspace\MyFirstPythonProject\src\FileOpeartions.py
Name of the file:  filedemo.txt
Hello Worl
Current file pointer position is  25
Current file pointer position is  0
Hello World!Hello Python!
```

Chapter 16
Exceptions Handling

Python language has two very important features to handle any unexpected error that may occur while executing the Python programs and to add debugging capabilities in them. Those features are as follows.

> **Exception Handling:** While writing a Python code, if we have a feeling that have some part of the code may raise an exception then we can handle that part by placing the code in a try: block. After the try: block, include an except: statement, followed by a block of code that handles the problem as effectively as possible. Syntax is given below.

try:

We do our operations here;

....

except Exception I:

If Exception I, then execute this block.

except Exception II:

If Exception II, then execute this block.

....

else: If no exception then execute this block.

Few points to remember about Python exception handling.

1. A single try statement can have multiple except statements. This feature can be well utilized when the try block contains statements that may throw more than one and different types of exceptions.

2. It supports feature to provide a generic except clause, which can handle any type of exception.

3. Syntactically, we can include an else-clause after the except clause(s). The code in the else-block will be executed only if the code in the try: block does not raise an exception.

4. The else-block is a useful programming place for code that does not need the try: block's protection.

Below is a list of standard Exceptions available in Python programming language.

EXCEPTION NAME	DESCRIPTION
Exception	This exception is the base class for all exceptions.
StopIteration	This exception is raised when the next () method of an iterator does not point to any object.
SystemExit	This exception is raised by the sys.exit () function.
StandardError	This exception is the base class for all built-in exceptions except SystemExit and StopIteration.
ArithmeticError	This exception is the base class for all errors that occur for numeric calculation.
OverflowError	This exception is raised when a calculation exceeds maximum limit for a numeric type.

FloatingPointError	This exception is raised when a floating point calculation fails.
ZeroDivisonError	This exception is raised when division or modulo by zero takes place for all numeric types.
AssertionError	This exception is raised in case of failure of the Assert statement.
AttributeError	This exception is raised in case of failure of attribute reference or assignment.
EOFError	This exception is raised when there is no input from either the raw_input () or input () function and the end of file is reached.
ImportError	This exception is raised when an import statement fails.
KeyboardInterrupt	This exception is raised when the user interrupts program execution, usually by pressing Ctrl+c.
LookupError	This exception is the base class for all lookup errors.
IndexError	Raised when an index is not found in a sequence.
KeyError	This exception is raised when the specified key is not found in the dictionary.
NameError	This exception is raised when an identifier is not found in the local or global namespace.
UnboundLocalError	This exception is raised when trying to access a local variable in a function or method but no value has been assigned to it.
EnvironmentError	This exception is the base class for all exceptions that occur outside the Python environment.
IOError	This exception is raised when an input/ output operation fails, such as the print statement or the open () function when trying to open a file that does not exist.
IOError	This exception is raised for operating system-related errors.
SyntaxError	This exception is raised when there is an error in Python syntax.
IndentationError	This exception is raised when indentation is not specified properly.

SystemError	This exception is raised when the interpreter finds an internal problem, but when this error is encountered the Python interpreter does not exit.
SystemExit	This exception is raised when Python interpreter is quit by using the sys.exit() function. If not handled in the code, causes the interpreter to exit.
ValueError	This exception is raised when the built-in function for a data type has the valid type of arguments, but the arguments have invalid values specified.
RuntimeError	This exception is raised when a generated error does not fall into any category.
NotImplementedError	This exception is raised when an abstract method that needs to be implemented in an inherited class is not actually implemented.

Python example on exception handling.

```
filedemo.txt    ExceptionHandling
1  # In this example testfile1.txt does not exists
2  try:
3      fileObject = open("testfile1.txt", "r")
4      fileObject.write("This is my test file that we are using for exception handling!!")
5  except IOError:
6      print ("Error: System can\'t find file or read data")
7  else:
8      print ("Content is written in the file successfully")
9      fileObject.close()

Console
<terminated> C:\Python_Workspace\MyFirstPythonProject\src\ExceptionHandling.py
Error: System can't find file or read data
```

The try-finally Clause

Finally is the block that comes at the last and is always executed irrespective of exception occurred or not. This is demonstrated in the below example.

```
filedemo.txt      ExceptionHandling ⊠
 1   # In this example testfile1.txt does not exist?
 2   try:
 3       fileObject = open("testfile1.txt", "r")
 4       fileObject.write("This is my test file that we are using for exception handling!!")
 5   except IOError:
 6       print ("Error: System can\'t find file or read data")
 7   else:
 8       print ("Content is written in the file successfully")
 9       fileObject.close()
10   finally:
11       print("We reached finally block")

 Console ⊠                                                          ▣ ✗ ✗ ⚬ ▦ | ▥ ▤
<terminated> C:\Python_Workspace\MyFirstPythonProject\src\ExceptionHandling.py
Error: System can't find file or read data
We reached finally block
```

> **Assertions:** An assertion in Python can be defined as a sanity-check that can turn on or turn off when we are done with the testing of the program. An expression is tested for the result, and if that comes up false, an exception is raised. Below is the syntax for assertions.

assert Expression[, Arguments]

If the assertion fails, Python will use an ArgumentExpression as the argument for the AssertionError. AssertionError is an exceptions that can be caught and handled like any other exception using the try-except statement If this exception is not handled, then it will terminate the program and produce a traceback as shown in the below example.

Given below is an example on Python Assertion, here, we are checking for account balance if it is lower than minimum balance of 5000. During first test for balance of 500, it passed the test therefore no AssertionError happened. However in the second case the input balance is 1000 which is less than minimum balance therefore AssertionError was raised in the console with our pre-defined message string (Account is in good condition above minimum balance).

```
Assertion ⊠
1  def account(balance):
2      assert (balance >= 5000),"Account is in good condition above minimum balance"
3      return balance
4  print (account(5000))
5  print (account(1000))
```

```
Console ⊠                                                          ▦ ✗ ✗ ✗ ✗
<terminated> C:\Python_Workspace\MyFirstPythonProject\src\Assertion.py
Traceback (most recent call last):
5000
  File "C:\Python_Workspace\MyFirstPythonProject\src\Assertion.py", line 5, in <module>
    print (account(1000))
  File "C:\Python_Workspace\MyFirstPythonProject\src\Assertion.py", line 2, in account
    assert (balance >= 5000),"Account is in good condition above minimum balance"
AssertionError: Account is in good condition above minimum balance
```

Chapter 17

Classes and Objects

Python is an object-oriented language from the day it exists. Let's take a quick revision on OOP (Object Oriented Programming) concepts.

OOP Concepts

- ➤ **Class:** A class is a user-defined prototype for an object that defines a set of attributes. The attributes are the data members (class or instance variables) and methods that are usually accessed via dot notation.

- ➤ **Class variable:** A class variable is the class reference that is shared by all instances of a class. Class variables are defined within a class but they are always outside any of the class's methods.

- ➤ **Data member:** It is a class or instance variable that holds data associated with a class and its objects.

- ➤ **Instance:** An individual object is an instance of a certain class.

- ➤ **Instantiation:** The creation of an instance of a class is called instantiation that creates a class object.

- ➤ **Method:** It is the name given to the function that is defined inside the class. It performs the actual operation on the variables.

- ➢ **Function overloading (Function Polymorphism):** Two or more functions with the same name but performing the different operation based on number of parameters, data type, etc.

- ➢ **Operator overloading (Operator Polymorphism):** A single operator has assignment of more than one function. E.g. '+' operator doing the mathematical addition of two numbers as well as concatenation of two strings.

- ➢ **Inheritance:** The transfer of the characteristics or traits from parent class to the child class. It encourages reusability.

- ➢ **Instance variable:** It is a variable that is defined inside a method and just belongs only to the current instance of a class.

- ➢ **Object:** It is a unique instance of a data structure (variables and methods) that's defined inside its class.

Creating Classes

In Python, the class statement creates a new class definition. It has the following syntax.

```
class ClassName:

    'Optional class documentation string'

    class_suite/component statements
```

- ➢ The class has an optional documentation string, which can be accessed via ClassName.__doc__.

> The class_suite consists of all the component statements that define class members, data attributes and functions.

Creating Instance Objects

An instance of class is created by calling the class using class name and pass in whatever arguments its __init__ method accepts.

Accessing Attributes

Attributes of the class can be accessed through the object's attributes using the dot operator with object.

Class demonstration in Python

In the below example, we are going to create a class and then instantiate its three objects to access their attributes.

```python
class Employee:
    'This is a Base class common for all employees'
    count = 0

    def __init__(self, empName, empSalary):
        self.name = empName
        self.salary = empSalary
        Employee.count += 1

    def displayCount(self):
        print ("Total Employee strength %d" % Employee.count)

    def displayEmployee(self):
        print ("Name of Employee : ", self.name,  ", Salary of Employee: ", self.salary)

# Instantiate a class object
"This would create first object of Employee class"
employee1 = Employee("Martin", "$30000")
employee2 = Employee("Julie", "$20000")
employee3 = Employee("Appy", "$90000")
# Accessing class attributes
employee1.displayEmployee()
employee2.displayEmployee()
employee3.displayEmployee()
print ("Total Employee %d" % Employee.count)
```

```
Name of Employee :  Martin , Salary of Employee:  $30000
Name of Employee :  Julie , Salary of Employee:  $20000
Name of Employee :  Appy , Salary of Employee:  $90000
Total Employee 3
```

Conclusion

Thank you again for downloading this book!

I hope this book was able to help you with getting started with Python! If it did I'd love to hear about it!

www.ingramcontent.com/pod-product-compliance
Lightning Source LLC
Chambersburg PA
CBHW071140050326
40690CB00008B/1519